THE BIG
BOTTOM
BISCUIT

the big bottom
BISCUIT

SPECIALTY BISCUITS
AND SPREADS FROM SONOMA'S

[big bottom market]

Michael Volpatt

RUNNING PRESS

PHILADELPHIA

Running Press
Hachette Book Group
1290 Avenue of the Americas,
New York, NY 10104
www.runningpress.com
@Running_Press

Printed in China

First Edition: April 2019

Published by Running Press, an imprint of Perseus Books, LLC, a subsidiary of Hachette Book Group, Inc. The Running Press name and logo is a trademark of the Hachette Book Group.

The Hachette Speakers Bureau provides a wide range of authors for speaking events. To find out more, go to www.hachettespeakersbureau.com or call (866) 376-6591

The publisher is not responsible for websites (or their content) that are not owned by the publisher.

Photography by Kelly Puleio

Print book cover and interior design by Frances J. Soo Ping Chow

Library of Congress Control Number: 2018961685

ISBNs: 978-0- 7624-6530-9 (hardcover), 978-0-7624-6531-6 (ebook)

1010

10 9 8 7 6 5 4 3 2 1

THIS BOOK IS DEDICATED TO **SUE STEINER**, THE "MOMMA" OF THE MARKET. YOU TRANSFORMED THE ORIGINAL BISCUIT RECIPE AND PUSHED ALL OF US TO BE CREATIVE. I'VE LEARNED SO MUCH FROM YOUR KITCHEN WISDOM AND AM FOREVER GRATEFUL FOR YOUR INSPIRATION.

CONTENTS

INTROD

This cookbook has been on my mind since my business partners and I opened Big Bottom Market steps away from the Russian River and Redwood Forest in the town of Guerneville, CA, in historic Sonoma wine country. After opening our doors, we quickly realized that guests loved our flavorful biscuits and were returning to the Market to both indulge in the classic version—made with our signature "wet" dough—and to try our other creative variations. Today, I'm proud to say we've served over 100,000 customers and sold tens of thousands of biscuits!

But before our little space transformed into what has become the heart of the Guerneville community, our kickoff team came up with the concept for the restaurant during long hikes in the Armstrong Redwoods State Natural Preserve just two miles outside our hamlet. We called the forest our "boardroom" and used it as a place for creativity and innovation. The history behind the massive trees made us realize that we needed to create a bit of our own lasting history in town. As a team we used the inspiration of the environment around us to come up with the idea for Big Bottom Market. In honor of the forest and the trees that inspired the opening of the market, we decided to name some of our menu items after the majestic redwoods. And it is here that the idea behind the biscuit was born.

WHAT'S IN A NAME?

The Big Bottom Market name celebrates the history of the area and our little town. Here's how it came about. . . . Our frequent hikes in the beautiful landscape of Armstrong Woods moved us to further explore the history behind the name of this amazing town where the market resides. We learned that modern-day Guerneville was first settled in 1860 on the bank of the Russian River in an alluvial flat known as Big Bottom, which became the name of the town. The area was sadly renamed Stumptown for its redwood logging and then changed to Guerneville in honor of the Guerne family. We decided it was time to take back the original name and celebrate the true settlement and history of the town, hence, Big Bottom Market. A unique, quirky, and historical description of the area that also suits the distinctive aspects and incredible environment we've created at the Market.

While our goal for the restaurant was to have a broad menu with gourmet sandwiches and salads (something that our town was sorely lacking), we also wanted to point to one thing about our eatery that we could call our own—something that would differentiate us, make us unique, and create a buzz. We scoured through recipe books, visited gourmet restaurants and storefronts and met with artisanal food purveyors and winemakers up and down the West Coast. Then one day it hit us—what could be made sweet or savory and loved by just about anyone? The biscuit.

This realization is when the research began—with the help of Christian Gomez we started testing recipes and tasting just about every type of biscuit we could make. The biscuit team—led by Sue Steiner, the momma of the Market and the woman that we've dedicated this book to—overwhelmingly agreed that the "wet biscuit" should be *our* biscuit. The wetness of the batter consistently ensured a fluffy biscuit while also allowing us to easily add all types of ingredients to further transform the recipe and make it our very own.

In 2011 we opened the doors and became known for our biscuit. People traveled from far and wide to taste our fluffy buttermilk morsels. The media got wind of our restaurant, too, and articles in local publications including *San Francisco* magazine, *Sonoma* magazine, the *San Francisco Chronicle*, and many more featured the market and talked about our biscuits.

With a background in PR, I wanted to get the most out of this early media and worked hard to see that we were consistently in the

Quite a bit actually...

Modern day Guerneville was first settled in 1860 on the bank of the Russian River on an alluvial flat known as **'Big Bottom'**. The area was sadly renamed Stumptown for its **redwood** logging. Our frequent hikes in the beautiful *landscape* moved us to further explore the history behind the name of this amazing town. The **unique,** quirky and inspiring description of the area not only fits the historical nature of days gone by, but also the distinctive aspects and **incredible environment** of the **market** you are about to

BIG BOTTOM WHITE 2016
SONOMA COUNTY

Wet stone, ginger flower, lime zest, tangerine, white peach. A note of
stone fruit and plenty of citrus accented by tucked-in florals on the
palate makes this an easy charmer and a dream when paired with food.
With hand-harvested and hand-sorted fruit sourced entirely from Estate
vineyards in the Chalk Hill district of Sonoma County, this wine was
literally born to pair with California Casual cuisine.

$19

[big bottom market]

BIG BOTTOM BUBBLES

Seville orange, market spice tea, bergamot, almond flower. Fine mousse
of tiny bubbles. Expressive, grown-up citrus fruit and spice on the palate
with a lengthy finish. Although individually a versatile wine equally
suited to sipping or pairing, this bottle is next-level delicious when
partnered with autumn and holiday dishes. Cheers!

$19

[big bottom market]

BIG BOTTOM RED 2014

Bright like a pinot and peppery like a zin. This overtly aromatic wine has
loud notes of ripe raspberry, strawberry and white pepper. Although
this 100% Grenache is lean, the palate is rich and warm. A tremendous
example of an estate Grenache grown in a cool climate.

$19

[big bottom market]

press, both locally and nationally. While we continued to enjoy much success, in 2016 we decided to partner with a few restaurants in New York City to see if including our biscuits on their brunch menus would prove successful. Customers loved them, and in response, we popped up the Big Bottom Biscuit Bar in the takeout window of Osteria Cotta on the Upper West Side, which caught the attention of numerous local media outlets including the *New York Times*. Once the *New York Times* came knocking, this was our signal that national expansion of our product was something we really needed to consider.

The Market's big break came on November 3, 2016, when our newly launched biscuit mix and honey was named one of "Oprah's Favorite Things." We quickly went from selling fifty bags of mix and jars of honey a month to more than six thousand of each in only six weeks. Collectively, our team ramped up production and pulled it off with the help of some locals and a relationship with Amazon.

It was around this time that my business partner and I decided that it was time to refocus our efforts and expand nationally. This decision led to a partnership with Zoe's Meats, a wholesale food company with warehouses and distribution relationships across the United States. In addition to now selling our mix and honey at several stores, we are also in the process of developing new products and further expanding our line into the food-service side of the business so that other bakeries and restaurants can also proudly serve Big Bottom Market products.

As if that weren't enough, we were also compelled to share our biscuit recipe with the world and give people a glimpse into our kitchen. Our goal was simple: let our guests and fans get a closer look at how our team works together to create our biscuits and the delicious recipes that complement and accompany them. What you hold in your hands right now is a dream come true and a labor of love for our entire team.

When people want to know what makes our biscuit just so special, I tell them it's that our easy-to-prepare biscuits take on a contemporary approach to the southern classic with a decidedly Northern California twist—and I don't know many people who can't resist a piping-hot biscuit. In this cookbook we've tried to elevate the biscuit with personal stories and unique recipes that have transformed our market and the way people eat our amazing biscuits. Within these pages you'll find more than fifty recipes for the biscuits,

butters, jams, and spreads that we prepare and serve at the Market. There are numerous recipes for specialty biscuits—always a customer favorite—that have everything from chocolate, bacon, and apples to all kinds of artisanal meats and locally sourced cheeses. You'll learn how to prepare some market favorites including The Sneaky (page 43), the Egg in a Biscuit (page 37), and the aptly named Sea Biscuit (page 32), with smoked salmon, crème fraîche, pickled onions, and capers. Rush to the Savory Embellishments section (page 104) for tasty dishes you may have never thought would pair well with the biscuit. We've even included dishes that actually incorporate leftover biscuits, such as the creative quiche recipes— the crust is made from day-old biscuits (page 148). What's the point here? The whole team worked and cooked our butts off to make sure there are a variety of recipes here to delight all tastes. And that is exactly what we've done in the pages ahead.

We do hope you will enjoy reading and preparing these recipes as much as we have loved the process of creating this beautiful cookbook.

A LITTLE BISCUIT HISTORY

The world's first biscuits were baked in Persia during the seventh century. What we think of as a biscuit today was a French invention. The French version is a twice-baked flat cookie or cake with a name derived from two Latin words—*bis* (twice) and *cuit* (cooked). Through the years, many nations have adapted the name and created their own version of the biscuit. In Italy, a biscotti is a hard "cookie" often served with espresso. The biscuit also has a strong identity in British culture as the traditional accompaniment to a cup of tea. The Brits are known for dunking biscuits—what we in the United States call a cookie—in tea so that they soften a little from the warmth of the liquid before being eaten.

For Americans, the biscuit is a quick bread, somewhat similar to a scone, and usually unsweetened (although we add sugar, and in many cases, as you will find in this book, other sweet indulgences). Self-rising flour—or flour with baking powder—is used to make the dough rise when baking in the oven. The North American version of the biscuit has its origins in the southern states, where generations have passed down family recipes.

We like to think that we are a new part of the biscuit's historical journey and evolution. Our version is a little wet, which makes it melt in your mouth and requires a preparation that is different from the southern style. To make it more "California," as we like to say, our team adds all sorts of sweet and savory ingredients. Of course, we always encourage our team to come up with their own versions; we hope you will take the base recipe and do the same. If you discover something you love, please share it with us on the Big Bottom Market Facebook page. Your creations just may make it onto our menu, and of course we will give you the credit you deserve.

TOOLS AND EQUIPMENT

You'll need a few simple ingredients and a handful of kitchen tools and equipment to concoct the perfect biscuit.

+ **8 X 8-INCH BAKING PAN**—If you don't have one already, get an 8 x 8-inch pan for baking your biscuits. We do not use pans that are coated with a nonstick surface; instead, we rely on cooking spray to ensure that the biscuits easily slide out of the pan when they're done cooking.

+ **DISPOSABLE PLASTIC GLOVES**—Since the batter can get messy, plastic gloves will keep your hands and batter nice and clean. We use gloves when combining the shortening with flour at the very beginning of recipe preparation.

+ **TOOTHPICKS, SKEWERS, OR A KNIFE**—These are used to ensure your biscuits are done before pulling them out of the oven. When your timer goes off, poke your cooked biscuits with one of these tools, and if it comes out clean they're done; if not, put them back in for another minute or two.

+ **ICE CREAM SCOOP**—You'll need an ice cream scoop to get the right amount of dough for each biscuit and to transfer the dough from the bowl to your baking pan (although a soup spoon also works). We use a 2.5-ounce scoop that we purchase online from a restaurant supply store, but you can also find one in your local kitchen store or in the grocery store. If you plan to make the Mini Biscuit recipe (page 22) you'll also want to get a 1.5- or 2-ounce scoop. Keep in mind you don't need to be a restaurant owner to shop for kitchen tools at a restaurant supply store. In fact, they are often less expensive and you can find pretty much everything you need to outfit the cook's perfect kitchen.

+ **INGREDIENTS**—While the ingredient list is short, the type of flour, sugar, honey, salt, shortening, buttermilk, and heavy cream will make a difference. You should always use self-rising flour because it has a leavening agent (baking powder to be exact) and you want your biscuits to rise up into fluffy little pastries. If you don't have self-rising flour we've included a recipe in the next paragraph that will show you how to make it on your own. Granulated sugar is a must for texture purposes. We use locally sourced honey and you should as well or head to the grocery and buy your favorite brand. Martha Stewart believes that kosher salt imparts a better flavor and we agree. Our team uses Diamond Crystal kosher salt. Shortening with no trans-fat is preferred, healthier for you, and not hard to find these days. Our dairy products, buttermilk and heavy cream, are sourced locally. We use low-fat buttermilk for no other reason than we think it tastes great and then cut the low-fat part out with the heavy cream!

Did you know that you can make your own self-rising flour? It's pretty easy. Combine 1 cup all-purpose flour with 1½ teaspoons baking powder and ½ teaspoon kosher salt. Stir until thoroughly mixed. We go through tons of self-rising flour at the Market and never concern ourselves with shelf life, but baking powder does lose its potency over time, which means your baked goods won't rise as they should. So unless you plan on making tons of biscuits (and we hope you do), consider this recipe as an alternative to purchasing a big bag and always check the date on your baking powder.

✦ Oven—Obviously you can't bake biscuits without an oven, but note that every oven is different. Temperature is very important when baking biscuits, so you may want to get an oven thermometer to test the temperature (especially when cooking with gas) before embarking on your biscuit bake. We use convection ovens at the Market and find that the internal fan helps to better distribute heat and bakes the biscuits more evenly.

THE ORIGINAL BIG BOTTOM BISCUIT

What Is a Wet Biscuit, Anyway?

At Big Bottom Market we make a wet biscuit, or what is traditionally known as a drop biscuit—the "dough" has a muffin or soft cookie batter look to it. First, we use an ice cream scoop to form the balls before tossing them with a little bit of flour. Then we nest them in a baking pan, one right next to the other, and as the biscuits bake in the oven they rise together. Dusting the batter with flour is key, because once the biscuits are done, the flour allows them to separate from each other easily. The resulting morsels have a rich, light-brown coloring on the outside and a melt-in-your-mouth warmth on the inside. You'll find over and over and over again throughout this book that this version of the biscuit goes well at any time of the day and with any meal. Is the biscuit the next donut or dinner roll with slightly more versatility? I'd argue yes, but I'll let you decide.

What It Means to "Nest" the Dough

Nesting is an important part of ensuring that the biscuits bake up properly. After you coat the biscuit in a little bit of flour, place the first biscuit in the corner of the pan. Place the following scoop of dough next to and slightly touching the first biscuit. Repeat until the pan is full. Note that every once in a while you might use a little too much batter for each of the biscuits and find yourself one or two biscuits short in your pan. If this happens take a piece of foil, roll it into a ball, spray with a little cooking spray, and use it as a placeholder

in the pan. Doing this will ensure that the biscuits rise up and not down into an empty space.

Everyone asks for our classic wet biscuit recipe, and for years we kept it hidden away. Before we opened the Market, our team tested and retested a number of recipes until we came up with our signature biscuit. Sue Steiner, the woman we call the momma of the Market and whom this book is dedicated to, deserves so much credit for her tenac-ity and creativity around everything biscuit. She taught us how to make the perfect biscuit and challenged us to further refine and evolve the recipe.

I recommend that you practice this base recipe a few times to ensure that you properly mix the shortening with the flour, sugar, and salt mixture, and also get the feel for the wetness of the dough. After you've perfected this recipe, move on to the others or use it as a base to come up with your own specialty creations.

The Original
Big Bottom Biscuit

Makes 9 biscuits

2¼ cups self-rising flour

⅛ cup granulated sugar

1 teaspoon kosher salt

2 tablespoons honey

¼ cup shortening

1 cup buttermilk

⅔ cup heavy cream

2 cups all-purpose flour

Preheat your oven to 400°F and coat an 8 x 8-inch baking pan with cooking spray.

Place the self-rising flour, sugar, salt, honey, and shortening in a large mixing bowl. Using your hands, blend the ingredients until the shortening is well combined and the mixture looks like small peas.

Add in the buttermilk and cream and stir with a spatula until fully combined. The dough will look wet and you may think there's not enough flour, but it's actually the wetness of the dough that makes the Big Bottom Market biscuit so moist and delicious. Trust me—don't add more.

Place the all-purpose flour in a medium-size mixing bowl. Use an ice-cream scoop to place one ball of wet dough into the flour. Toss the ball around so the flour coats the dough and then place it into the baking pan. Do this until all of the dough is gone, being sure to nest the biscuits one next to the other so that they all just barely touch in the pan.

Bake for 20 minutes on the top rack. After 20 minutes, turn the pan 180 degrees and bake for another 5 to 10 minutes. After 5 minutes, check for doneness with a toothpick. If it comes out clean and the tops are golden brown, your biscuits are ready. If not, bake for up to an additional 5 minutes and check again. Every oven is different so baking times may vary.

Remove from the oven and let cool in the pan for 10 to 15 minutes before serving.

VARIATION: Using a small spoon or smaller ice cream scoop, you can make what we call the Mini Biscuit. This is simply a smaller version of the basic biscuit and is a great snack to pop into your mouth or use for appetizers, dips, and spreads. After coating an 8 x 8-inch pan with cooking spray, scoop out the mix into the pan while nesting the balls one next to the other in the same way as you did with the larger sized biscuits. You should end up with about 25 biscuits in the pan. Bake at the same temperature—400°F—and after 15 minutes, turn the pan 180° and bake for another 5 to 10 minutes. Check for doneness with a toothpick. If it comes out clean and the tops are golden brown, your biscuits are ready. Before serving, let them cool and then top with some of the amazing spreads from the Butters, Jams, Spreads, and More chapter on page 72.

A note on eliminating trans fat:

Trans fats, a naughty word these days in many cooking and nutrition circles, are created in an industrial process that adds hydrogen to liquid vegetable oils to make them more solid. These "partially hydrogenated oils" are in many of the processed foods we eat today, but thankfully, this is slowly beginning to change.

In the interest of creating the best biscuit and in trying to keep our guests' and readers' health in mind, our team has eliminated the use of partially hydrogenated trans fat shortening from our biscuit recipes. When making the recipes in this book, we also want to encourage you to stay away from shortening with trans fat. Your heart will thank you, and so will your friends and family as they gobble biscuits up!

SPEC
BISC

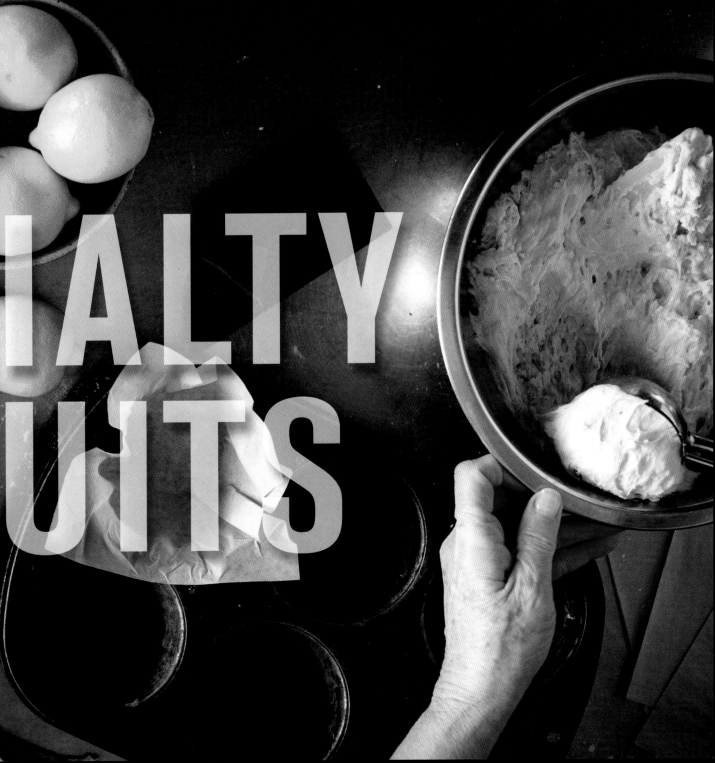

While the Big Bottom Market biscuit already tastes sublime as is, we couldn't help getting creative and evolving the recipe beyond the classic biscuit. Our team has spent hours coming up with unique concoctions and creative variations that wow our guests and keep them coming back for more.

In this chapter, you'll find everything from sweet and savory to some fancy, flavorful, and mouthwatering biscuit sandwiches. We're also revealing our very own version of gravy that we top the biscuits with and use in scrumptious biscuit pot pies (page 156).

Look around your kitchen. Think about flavor pairings that make your mouth water, and you are well on your way to coming up with your very own specialty biscuits. Let's say you want to make a Havarti dill biscuit: it's not hard at all. Use the 2-cup biscuit recipe that you'll find in many of the recipes in this chapter as your base. Then add in ⅓ cup grated Havarti cheese and a tablespoon of fresh dill. Follow the baking directions for any of the 2-cup recipe specialty biscuits and you are all set. Or what about a banana coconut biscuit? The 2-cup recipe is your base again, but this time add in ⅓ cup chopped banana and ⅓ cup shredded coconut, bake according to the recipe directions, and voilà—your biscuits are ready. You can even make your own sweet and savory toppings to finish your creations off. Just make sure you let your biscuits cool down a little before adding on any toppings so they don't melt into the dough.

It's Cheddar Thyme

When we first opened the market we offered two types of biscuits—plain and cheddar thyme. People loved the cheddar thyme so much that we started exploring other flavors and soon realized that the specialty biscuit could be so much more. That is when we began introducing new flavors, both sweet and savory, into our daily offerings. This original recipe, with its combination of cheddar cheese and fresh thyme, is still a favorite.

Makes 6 biscuits

2 cups self-rising flour

¼ cup granulated sugar

1 teaspoon salt

¼ cup shortening

1 cup buttermilk

⅔ cup cream

½ cup grated white cheddar cheese, divided

1 tablespoon fresh thyme

Preheat your oven to 400°F.

Place the flour, sugar, salt, and shortening in a large bowl. Using your hands, blend the ingredients until the shortening is well combined and the mixture looks like small peas.

Add in the buttermilk and cream along with ¼ cup cheese and the thyme. Stir with a spatula until fully combined.

Spray a six-cup jumbo muffin tin and six pieces of 5 x 5-inch parchment paper with cooking spray. Then place the pieces of parchment paper on top of the muffin cups and place a large scoop of biscuit batter on each of the parchment papers. The batter and the paper will fall to the bottom of each compartment. Top each dough ball with cheese from the remaining ¼ cup.

Bake for 20 minutes until the cheese on top has melted and is golden brown. Poke a toothpick into the center of the biscuit; if it comes out clean, the biscuits are done. If not, bake for an additional 5 minutes.

Remove from the oven and let cool for 15 to 20 minutes before serving.

The Fairy Biscuit

The idea for this biscuit came from an Aussie friend of mine. One day he asked me if we ever make fairy toast at the market. "Um . . . what?" He went on to explain that fairy bread, loved by Australian kids everywhere, is sliced white bread spread with butter and covered with hundreds and thousands, which stick to the butter. Apparently, in Australia, "hundreds and thousands" are what we call sprinkles. So we created this biscuit version that kids and sweet-tooth adults absolutely love. We even secure the sprinkles on top of the biscuits using sweet "fairy glue," which you'll learn how to make in this tasty recipe.

Makes 6 biscuits

2 cups self-rising flour

½ teaspoon kosher salt

¼ cup granulated sugar

¼ cup shortening

1 cup buttermilk

⅔ cup heavy cream

1 tablespoon fresh thyme (you can substitute 1 teaspoon dried, but fresh is always better)

1 (10.5-ounce) jar hundreds and thousands (A.K.A. sprinkles), divided

For the Fairy Glue:

1 cup confectioners' sugar

3 tablespoons heavy cream

⅛ teaspoon vanilla extract

Preheat your oven to 400°F.

Place the flour, salt, granulated sugar, and shortening in a large bowl. Using your hands, blend the ingredients until the shortening is well combined and the mixture looks like small peas.

Add in the buttermilk and cream and then ¼ cup hundreds and thousands. Stir with a spatula until fully combined. Your batter will likely become purple. Don't worry— fairies, children, and fearless adults love purple batter.

Spray a 6-cup jumbo muffin tin and six pieces of 5 x 5-inch parchment paper with cooking spray. Then place the parchment paper on top of the muffin tin and place a large scoop of biscuit batter on each of the parchment papers. The batter and the paper will fall to the bottom of each cup.

Bake for 25 minutes. Poke a toothpick into the center of the biscuit; if it comes out clean, the biscuits are done. If not, bake for an additional 5 minutes.

Remove from the oven and let cool for 15 to 20 minutes before serving.

To make the sweet fairy glue, mix together the confectioners' sugar, cream, and vanilla until the mixture is the consistency of a thick paste.

Once the biscuits have cooled, slather the top of each biscuit with fairy glue. Next you'll be sprinkling the remaining hundreds and thousands on top. To insure that they don't go all over the floor, place one of the biscuits into a sieve and sprinkle the hundreds and thousands onto the top of the biscuit until fully covered. Empty the sieve back into the jar and repeat with the rest of the biscuits. Be sure to serve the kiddos before *any* adult gets his or her hands on these sweet treats.

The Sea Biscuit

As we were planning the menu for the market and preparing to open our doors, the team tested a number of biscuit variations and sandwiches while also seeking feedback from our friends and future guests. My good friend Jonathan Teel—a foodie in his own right—came up with the idea for a specialty sea biscuit, and it continues to be one of our most popular menu items. So when we popped up the Big Bottom Biscuit Bar in New York City we decided that our marketing tactic would be to take on an NYC favorite. Our tagline was, "Watch out bagel and lox, the Sea Biscuit has arrived." It was a fun way to draw attention to a new version of something that is a classic breakfast staple in the Big Apple. For further fun, check out the section on how to create your own biscuit bar on page 140. The biscuit bar is great for parties and gives your brunch, lunch, or dinner guests everything they need to make their very own Sea Biscuit and beyond.

Makes 9 biscuits

9 Original Big Bottom Biscuits (page 20)

¾ cup pickled red onions (about 1 tablespoon per biscuit), recipe below

1 pound smoked salmon (about 2 ounces per biscuit)

¾ cup crème fraîche (about 1 tablespoon per biscuit)

9 tablespoons capers

For the pickled onions:

1 large red onion

½ cup white vinegar

⅓ cup granulated sugar

¼ teaspoon crushed red pepper flakes

⅛ cup kosher salt

1 bay leaf

½ of a cinnamon stick

Start by preparing the biscuits (page 20).

While the biscuits are baking, make the pickled onions.

Thinly slice the onion using a mandoline. Place all the ingredients into a saucepan with ½ cup water and bring to a boil, about 2 minutes. Remove from the heat and let cool to room temperature. Transfer into a jar with a lid, and place in the refrigerator.

Split each biscuit in half and place about 2 ounces of the smoked salmon (this comes out to about two pieces from the fillet of salmon) onto the bottom of each biscuit. Top with 1 tablespoon crème fraîche, 1 tablespoon pickled onions, 1 teaspoon capers, and then put the top on. You now have a Sea Biscuit sandwich, and yes, it is that easy.

VARIATION: It's easy to make the Sea Biscuit even fancier and tastier than it already is. White Sturgeon Caviar farmed in the United States is not only affordable but also delicious. One-ounce jars of caviar will net you about 6 teaspoons, so get 3 jars for 9 servings. I like to place about 2 teaspoons of caviar on the top of the Sea Biscuit to finish it off. Serving this dish with a glass of sparkling wine from the Russian River or your favorite champagne is an ideal and decadent accompaniment.

The Claw and Slaw

This recipe brings together three of my favorite things: crabmeat, tarragon, and my friend Jonathan. My parents often serve a dish called Crabmeat Hoelzel that hails from the kitchens of the Duquesne Club in Pittsburgh, PA. While working with Jonathan our team decided to create a version of Hoelzel by replacing jumbo lump crabmeat from the East Coast with Dungeness crab from the West. The slaw in this recipe elegantly integrates the tarragon and results in a flavorful combination that pairs well with the biscuit. We serve our version with a little side of greens and a simple vinaigrette.

Makes 8 biscuits

8 Original Big Bottom Biscuits (page 20)
1 pound Dungeness crabmeat (you can also use jumbo lump crabmeat)

For the slaw:
⅓ cup extra-virgin olive oil
⅔ cup rice vinegar
1 tablespoon honey
⅓ cup chopped fresh tarragon
1 teaspoon kosher salt
1 teaspoon freshly ground black pepper
7 cups slaw mix (equal parts carrots, red cabbage, and green cabbage)

Start by preparing the biscuits (page 20).

In a large bowl, whisk together the olive oil, vinegar, honey, tarragon, salt, and pepper. Add in the chopped slaw mix and stir well. Cover and refrigerate until ready to serve.

To assemble, cut a cooled biscuit in half and place the bottom into a bowl and set the top aside. Top with about ½ cup slaw and 2 ounces crabmeat.

NOTE: Make your life easier and buy a bag of prechopped slaw mix from the grocery store. A 10-ounce bag will yield about 7 cups of slaw.

Egg in a Biscuit

This recipe is a classic favorite at the market and one popularized by Momma Sue. Have you ever had a Scotch Egg (a hard-boiled egg wrapped in sausage meat, coated in breadcrumbs, and baked or deep fried)? Egg in a Biscuit is a play on the Scotch Egg but has a biscuity soft outer layer that melts in your mouth with what ends up looking like a hard-boiled egg in the center. While that may sound challenging, it is actually very easy!

Makes 6 biscuits

2 cups self-rising flour

½ teaspoon kosher salt

¼ cup sugar

¼ cup shortening

1 cup buttermilk

⅔ cup heavy cream

6 large eggs

⅓ cup shredded cheddar cheese

Preheat your oven to 400°F.

Place the flour, salt, sugar, and shortening in a large bowl. Using your hands, blend the ingredients until the shortening is well combined and the mixture looks like small peas. Add in the buttermilk and cream and stir with a spatula until fully combined.

Spray a 6-cup jumbo muffin tin and six pieces of 5 x 5-inch parchment paper with cooking spray. Then place the pieces of parchment paper on top of the muffin cups and place a large scoop of biscuit batter on each of the parchment papers. The batter and the paper will fall to the bottom of each compartment.

Bake for 15 minutes and remove from the oven.

Bore a quarter-size hole about halfway down into the partially cooked biscuit with the clean handle of a wooden spoon. Then crack an egg into a small bowl and pour one in each of the holes. Top each biscuit with some of the cheddar cheese and place back in the oven. Bake for an additional 10 minutes. Check doneness by poking the biscuit and the egg. If both come out clean, remove from the oven. You can tell that the egg is done if the watery part of the egg (the albumin) surrounding the yolk is white on top of the biscuit. If not, bake for another 5 minutes.

Let cool for 15 to 20 minutes before serving.

VARIATION: I like using cheddar cheese for this recipe, but you can choose any melty and delicious cheese that you want. Try Monterey Jack, Asiago, Blue Cheese, or pretty much anything that melts well and tastes great.

Mexican Omelet Biscuit

Theresa is our cook at the market and not only brings her A-game each and every day she steps into the kitchen, she also brings her special knowledge of Mexican cuisine and culture. We encourage her to look through cookbooks and work up her own recipes that she thinks our customers will love, and incorporate her family recipes and Mexican heritage into what she creates. This savory biscuit that Theresa dreamed up is deliciously flavorful and inspired by the bold ingredients that Mexican cooking has to offer.

Makes 6 biscuits

1 tablespoon extra-virgin olive oil
½ medium yellow onion, diced
½ medium red bell pepper, diced
1 tablespoon diced jalapeño
3 large eggs
2 cups self-rising flour
½ teaspoon kosher salt
¼ cup granulated sugar
¼ cup shortening
1 cup buttermilk
⅔ cup heavy cream
2 tablespoons chopped fresh cilantro
Zest from 1 lime (about 1 teaspoon)

Preheat your oven to 400°F.

Place the olive oil in a medium-size pan and sauté the onion, pepper, and jalapeño over medium heat, until the onion is translucent, for 2 to 3 minutes.

In a bowl, crack the eggs, mix with a whisk, and pour into the pan with the veggie mixture. Using a spatula, fold the eggs into the veggie mix and cook until the eggs are done. This should take 3 to 5 minutes. Set aside to cool and break up into smaller pieces with a spatula.

Place the flour, salt, sugar, and shortening in a large bowl. Using your hands, blend the ingredients until the shortening is well combined and the mixture looks like small peas.

Add in the buttermilk, cream, egg mixture, cilantro, and lime zest and stir with a spatula until fully combined.

Spray a 6-cup jumbo muffin tin and six pieces of 5 x 5-inch parchment paper with cooking spray. Then place the parchment paper on top of the muffin tin and place a large scoop of biscuit batter on each of the parchment papers. The batter and paper will fall to the bottom of each compartment.

Bake in the oven for 20 minutes. Poke a toothpick into the center of the biscuit. If it comes out clean it is done. If not, bake for an additional 5 minutes.

Let cool for 15 to 20 minutes before serving.

VARIATION: Spicy foods can be a bit of a problem for me and my tummy, so I go easy on the jalapeños. If you really want to spice this up, however, you can add more jalapeño and include the seeds—that's where the heat is most powerful.

NOTE: One of the best ways to bring freshness into a recipe is to add citrus zest to the dish right when you are about to serve it. Lemon, lime, and orange zest all play a role in many of the foods we create at the Market; each imparts its own intense citrus flavor with very little bitterness. The bitter part of citrus fruits is found in the white part or pith of the fruit, which is thankfully not part of the zest. For another recipe with zest, check out the recipe for gremolata on page 120. This is one of the best uses of zest and really helps to elevate the overall flavor profile for many of the biscuit recipes in this book.

The Sneaky

The Sneaky is our version of a sausage, egg, and cheese biscuit. We call it The Sneaky, because every once in a while, Donna, our working partner and general manager at the Market, and I sneak out to a not-to-be-named fast food restaurant to indulge in the same sandwich. We thought we'd create our own version and people *loved* it. The trick with this one is to make sure that the cheese melts on top of the sausage, so get your broiler ready to roll as you prepare this tasty sandwich.

Makes 9 biscuits

9 Original Big Bottom Biscuits (page 20)

1¼ pounds ground sausage (you can use sweet or hot)

¾ cup Lemon Garlic Aioli (page 99)

9 hard-boiled eggs, peeled and sliced (this is best done with an egg slicer)

9 slices of cheddar cheese

Start by preparing the biscuits (page 20).

While the biscuits are baking, prepare the sausage patties. Form the sausage into 2-ounce patties and cook in a frying pan on medium heat for 3 to 5 minutes on each side. Set aside.

Turn the oven broiler on high.

When the biscuits are ready and have cooled, slice each in half and spread aioli on each side. Place the sausage patties on the bottom half of each biscuit. Place egg slices on top of each of the sausage patties. Top with a slice of cheddar cheese and place the bottom halves only on a cookie sheet and then under the broiler. Keep an eye on the cheese so it doesn't burn. Once melted, remove from the oven, top with the other biscuit halves, and serve that Sneaky to friends and family.

VARIATION: Plant-based "meats" seem to be all the rage these days. They are made to look, taste, and also "bleed" like beef burgers, and many of these products have done a good job of replicating the flavor profile too. One brand actually uses beet extract to create the bleeding effect that you get from red meat. Getting your hands on one of these "meat" products is pretty easy. If you are a vegetarian, vegan, or watching your intake of meat products, substitute a plant-based patty for the sausage.

The S'mores Biscuit

Theresa (the market's expert biscuit baker) and I were brainstorming specialty biscuit recipes one day. As we were coming up with tasty concepts I blurted out, "S'mores biscuit!" and she replied that she'd never had a S'more before. I was so astounded that we immediately ran out and grabbed marshmallows, graham crackers, and chocolate chips, and hurried back to bake 'em up. This biscuit recipe brings back memories of marshmallows on the end of a stick melting over a hot campfire and then being smashed with graham crackers and chocolate. So good.

Makes 6 biscuits

2 cups self-rising flour

½ teaspoon kosher salt

¼ cup granulated sugar

¼ cup shortening

1 cup buttermilk

⅔ cup heavy cream

½ cup mini marshmallows, plus extra for garnish

⅓ cup semisweet chocolate chips

½ cup graham cracker crumbs plus extra for garnish

Creamy chocolate topping, for drizzling (page 53)

Preheat the oven to 400°F.

Place the flour, salt, sugar, and shortening in a large bowl. Using your hands, blend the ingredients until the shortening is well combined and the mixture looks like small peas.

Add in the buttermilk, cream, marshmallows, chocolate chips, and graham cracker crumbs and stir until well combined.

Spray a 6-cup jumbo muffin tin and six pieces of 5 x 5-inch parchment paper with cooking spray. Then place the parchment paper on top of the muffin tin and place a large scoop of biscuit batter on each of the parchment papers. The batter and the paper will fall to the bottom of each compartment.

Place in the oven and bake for 25 minutes. Poke a toothpick into the center of the biscuit and if it comes out clean it is done. If not, then bake for an additional 5 minutes. Let cool for 15 to 20 minutes.

Drizzle the top of each biscuit with creamy chocolate topping, some more marshmallows, and a sprinkle of graham cracker crumbs, and serve.

VARIATION: If you want to evoke even more memories by the campfire, brûlée the tops of your marshmallows with a chef's torch before placing them on the chocolate topping and sprinkling with the graham cracker crumbs.

The Saucy Italian

My whole family—mom, dad, sister, brother, and cousins—inspire me in the kitchen. Our heritage and cooking style is deeply rooted in Northern Italy, and I've done my best to integrate some of the Volpatt family favorites into specialty items at the Market. This Saucy Italian takes the specialty biscuit to a tasty new level with an inspired version of my mother's easy-to-make marinara sauce while the addition of gremolata gives it a fresh and light taste.

Makes 6 biscuits

2 cups self-rising flour

½ teaspoon kosher salt

¼ cup granulated sugar

¼ cup shortening

1 cup buttermilk

⅔ cup heavy cream

⅓ cup chopped pepperoni (I prefer using presliced and roughly chopping)

⅓ cup grated Parmesan

⅓ cup shredded mozzarella, plus extra to top the biscuits

For the marinara sauce:

Extra-virgin olive oil

½ yellow onion, chopped

3 garlic cloves, minced

2 teaspoons kosher salt

2 teaspoons freshly ground black pepper

½ cup dry vermouth

1 (28-ounce) can Italian-style peeled tomatoes (I prefer the Simpson Imports San Marzano brand, which are available at most grocery stores, in a white can)

½ cup grated Parmesan

Zest from ½ lemon (about 1 teaspoon)

½ cup chopped fresh parsley

6 tablespoons gremolata (page 120)

Preheat your oven to 400°F.

Place the flour, salt, sugar, and shortening in a large bowl. Using your hands, blend the ingredients until the shortening is well combined and the mixture looks like small peas.

Add in the buttermilk, cream, pepperoni, and cheeses. Stir with a spatula until fully combined.

Spray a 6-cup jumbo muffin tin and six pieces of 5 x 5-inch parchment paper with cooking spray. Place the parchment paper on top of the muffin tin and place a large scoop of biscuit batter on each of the parchment papers. The batter and the paper will fall to the bottom of each cup. Top each dough ball with a few shreds of mozzarella.

Bake in the oven for 20 minutes. Poke a toothpick into the center of the biscuit and if it comes out clean it is done. If not, then bake for an additional 5 minutes. Let cool for 15 to 20 minutes before assembling and serving.

While the biscuits are cooking, prepare the marinara sauce. Cover the bottom of a medium-size saucepan with the olive oil. Turn the heat to medium and add in the onions. Sauté for 3 to 5 minutes, stirring constantly until the onions are translucent. Then add in the garlic and sauté for another 1 to 2 minutes. You will begin to smell the beautiful scent of cooking garlic fill the air. Add in the salt, pepper, and vermouth and let the vermouth cook down by half.

Blend the tomatoes in a blender or food processor and add to the saucepan. Let the sauce cook on medium heat for 15 to 20 minutes. Remove from the heat and add in the Parmesan, zest, and parsley.

Give the sauce a taste and add additional salt and pepper as necessary.

To serve, cover the bottom of six medium-size bowls with marinara sauce. Place a biscuit on top of the sauce in each bowl. Add more sauce on top of the biscuit if you want it really saucy. Then finish it off with a teaspoon or so of the gremolata on top of each biscuit and serve.

Fig Jam and Goat Cheese Biscuit

My friends on Fire Island and I have a little game we play with one another the morning after a big dinner party, where we see who can come up with the most inventive use for last night's leftovers. We're all pretty creative. In an effort to ensure that we are repurposing ingredients in creative ways at the Market, we've adopted a similar strategy. We always try to repurpose foods we already have in the kitchen. The jam for this biscuit is the same one we use in our fig and prosciutto sandwich and pairs very well with the savory zing of goat cheese. While we don't make our own fig jam at the Market—because finding good figs can be a challenge when not in season—you can easily head to your local gourmet store or online to find the perfect fig jam for this recipe. We use a locally sourced product called Inna Jam, which we love and is available online.

Makes 6 biscuits

2 cups self-rising flour

½ teaspoon kosher salt

¼ cup granulated sugar

¼ cup shortening

1 cup buttermilk

⅔ cup heavy cream

2 tablespoons fig jam

1 tablespoon goat cheese,
plus extra to top the biscuits

Honey, for drizzling

Preheat your oven to 400°F.

Place the flour, salt, sugar, and shortening in a large bowl. Using your hands, blend the ingredients until the shortening is well combined and the mixture looks like small peas.

Add the buttermilk, cream, fig jam, and 1 tablespoon goat cheese to the biscuit mix and stir until well combined.

Spray a 6-cup jumbo muffin tin and six pieces of 5 x 5-inch parchment paper with cooking spray. Then place the parchment paper on top of the muffin tin and place a large scoop of biscuit batter on each of the parchment papers. The batter and the paper will fall to the bottom of each cup.

Place in the oven and bake for 25 minutes. Poke a toothpick into the center of the biscuit and if it comes out clean it is done. If not, then bake for an additional 5 minutes. Let cool for 15 to 20 minutes.

Drizzle the top of each biscuit with honey, top with crumbled goat cheese, and serve.

The Aphrodisiac Biscuit

For Valentine's Day, we decided it'd be fun to do some research on sexy foods that are known to spark a little romance in the bedroom, with a reputation for inspiring love and fertility. The end result? This amazing Aphrodisiac Biscuit made with dark chocolate and dried cherries. Although the jury is still out as to whether cherries and chocolate truly spark attraction, we do know that people love the combination—especially when slathered with creamy chocolate topping.

Makes 6 biscuits

2 cups self-rising flour

½ teaspoon kosher salt

¼ cup granulated sugar

¼ cup shortening

1 cup buttermilk

⅔ cup heavy cream

⅓ cup chopped dried cherries

⅓ cup chopped dark chocolate

For the creamy chocolate topping:

1 cup semisweet chocolate chips

¼ cup heavy cream

1 teaspoon light corn syrup

Preheat the oven to 400°F.

Place the flour, salt, sugar, and shortening in a large bowl. Using your hands, blend the ingredients until the shortening is well combined and the mixture looks like small peas.

Add the buttermilk, cream, cherries, and chocolate to the biscuit mix and stir until well combined. Spray a 6-cup jumbo muffin tin and six pieces of 5 x 5-inch parchment paper with cooking spray. Then place the parchment paper on top of the muffin tin and place a large scoop of biscuit batter on each of the parchment papers. The batter and the paper will fall to the bottom of each cup.

Place in the oven and bake for 20 minutes. Poke a toothpick into the center of the biscuit and if it comes out clean it is done. If not, then bake for an additional 5 minutes. Let cool for 15 to 20 minutes.

While the biscuits are cooling, prepare the creamy chocolate topping. Place the chocolate chips, cream, and corn syrup in a microwave-safe bowl. Microwave on high for about 30 seconds. Remove, stir, and if it is too thick, add another tablespoon of cream. If it is too thin, add a tablespoon more of chocolate chips. Microwave again for 15 to 20 seconds, remove, and spread on top of the biscuits.

Strawberry Cream Biscuit

We used to serve this biscuit like a strawberry shortcake—we'd dice fresh strawberries, make homemade whipped cream, and serve the two on top of a biscuit with some mint as garnish. In the interest of time and to simplify prep work in the kitchen we decided to add the ingredients right into the biscuit, and what resulted is a super tasty, three-bite strawberry shortcake that you can hold right in your hand, complete with creamy frosting right on top.

Makes 6 biscuits

2 cups self-rising flour

½ teaspoon kosher salt

¼ cup granulated sugar

¼ cup shortening

1 cup buttermilk

⅔ cup heavy cream

2 tablespoons cream cheese frosting, plus extra for the tops (recipe below)

⅓ cup chopped strawberries, plus 3 additional whole strawberries cut in half

For the cream cheese frosting:

4 ounces cream cheese, at room temperature

1 cup confectioners' sugar

4 tablespoons heavy cream

½ teaspoon vanilla extract

Prepare the cream cheese frosting first. Combine the cream cheese frosting ingredients in a mixing bowl. Using a hand mixer (or a standing mixer with paddle attachment), blend the ingredients together until the mixture has the consistency of frosting. You can add in more confectioners' sugar if it is too thin or more cream if it is too thick. Place in the refrigerator.

Preheat the oven to 400°F.

Place the flour, salt, granulated sugar, and shortening in a large bowl. Using your hands, blend the ingredients until the shortening is well combined and the mixture looks like small peas.

Add the buttermilk, cream, 2 tablespoons of cream cheese frosting, and the chopped strawberries to the biscuit mix. Stir with a spatula until fully combined.

Spray a 6-cup jumbo muffin tin and six pieces of 5 x 5-inch parchment paper with cooking spray. Then place the parchment paper on top of the muffin tin and place a large scoop of biscuit batter on each of the parchment papers. The batter and the paper will fall to the bottom of each cup.

Place in the oven and bake for 20 minutes. Poke a toothpick into the center of the biscuit and if it comes out clean it is done. If not, then bake for an additional 5 minutes. Let cool for 15 to 20 minutes. Once cool, top with the remaining frosting and half of a strawberry.

Chocolate Bacon Biscuit

Just about everybody loves bacon. Our most requested breakfast sandwich at the Market is the Bacon Brekky with bacon, hard-boiled egg, cheddar, spinach, garlic, and aioli, warmed and pressed on ciabatta. We also sell bacon and chocolate candy bars, and people are always asking us if they can top their biscuits and gravy with bacon. So we created a chocolate bacon biscuit, which has become one of our most popular specialties. The sweetness of the chocolate and saltiness from the bacon are an absolute perfect combination.

Makes 6 biscuits

2 cups self-rising flour

½ teaspoon kosher salt

¼ cup granulated sugar

¼ cup shortening

1 cup buttermilk

⅔ cup heavy cream

3 strips cooked bacon, chopped (⅓ cup), plus 1 strip cooked and cut into six pieces for garnish

⅓ cup semisweet chocolate chips

Preheat the oven to 400°F.

Place the flour, salt, sugar, and shortening in a large bowl. Using your hands, blend the ingredients until the shortening is well combined and the mixture looks like small peas.

Add the buttermilk, cream, chopped bacon, and chocolate chips to the biscuit mix and stir until well combined.

Spray a 6-cup jumbo muffin tin and six pieces of 5 x 5-inch parchment paper with cooking spray. Then place the parchment paper on top of the muffin tin and place a large scoop of biscuit batter on each of the parchment papers. The batter and the paper will fall to the bottom of each cup.

Place in the oven and bake for 20 minutes. Poke a toothpick into the center of the biscuit and if it comes out clean it is done. If not, then bake for an additional 5 minutes.

Remove from the oven and while warm, top each biscuit with a piece of bacon.

Wild Berry Crumble

In the summertime all over Western Sonoma County, there is an abundance of wild blackberries. In my backyard, along hiking trails, and even in the "urban" areas of our little hamlet you can find deliciously sweet wild berries growing all over the place. Oftentimes we will harvest the berries and use them to make a berry-inspired biscuit. While you may not have wild berries at your disposal, you can always visit your local farmers' market or gourmet store and "handpick" the sweetest ones you can find. Don't be afraid to use frozen berries, but make sure you thaw them and drain the excess juice before baking them into your biscuits. The extra juice adds too much liquid to the batter and you'll end up with really wet dough that won't bake properly.

Makes 6 biscuits

2 cups self-rising flour

½ teaspoon kosher salt

¼ cup granulated sugar

¼ cup shortening

1 cup buttermilk

⅔ cup heavy cream

½ cup frozen or fresh blackberries or raspberries, thawed and drained if frozen

For the crumble:

1 cup all-purpose flour

½ cup light brown sugar

¼ cup (½ stick) butter, at room temperature

1 teaspoon vanilla extract

1 teaspoon ground cinnamon

¼ teaspoon kosher salt

Preheat the oven to 400°F.

Place the flour, salt, granulated sugar, and shortening in a large bowl. Using your hands, blend the ingredients until the shortening is well combined and the mixture looks like small peas.

Add the buttermilk, cream, and raspberries to the biscuit mix and stir until well combined. Set aside and prepare the crumble topping.

Combine all the ingredients for the crumble in a bowl, mix until well combined, and set aside.

Spray a 6-cup jumbo muffin tin and six pieces of 5 x 5-inch parchment paper with cooking spray. Then place the parchment paper on top of the muffin tin and place a large scoop of biscuit batter on each of the parchment papers. The batter and the paper will fall to the bottom of each cup.

Sprinkle each biscuit with some of the crumb topping, place in the oven, and bake for 20 minutes. Poke a toothpick into the center of the biscuit and if it comes out clean it is done. If not, then bake for an additional 5 minutes. Let cool for 15 to 20 minutes.

Sweet and Sour

This lemon curd biscuit is sweet and tart all at the same time, as well as absolutely delicious. I love making lemon curd. It's not only easy to make, it also stores well in the refrigerator for about a week. After using it in this recipe, if there is any leftover, you can drizzle it on top of ice cream, or top your pancakes with lemon curd instead of syrup. Make extra and I promise you won't be sorry!

Makes 6 biscuits

2 cups self-rising flour

½ teaspoon kosher salt

¼ cup granulated sugar

¼ cup shortening

1 cup buttermilk

⅔ cup heavy cream

1 cup fresh or frozen blueberries, plus more for garnish

2 tablespoons confectioners' sugar

2 egg whites

6 fresh mint leaves, for garnish

For the lemon curd:

¾ cup fresh lemon juice
(about 3 or 4 medium lemons)

Zest from 2 medium lemons
(2½ teaspoons; zest lemons prior
to squeezing for juice)

1 cup granulated sugar

4 large eggs

½ cup (1 stick) unsalted butter

Preheat the oven to 400°F.

Place the flour, salt, granulated sugar, and shortening in a large bowl. Using your hands, blend the ingredients until the shortening is well combined and the mixture looks like small peas.

Add the buttermilk, cream, and 1 cup of blueberries to the biscuit mix and stir until well combined.

Spray a 6-cup jumbo muffin tin and six pieces of 5 x 5-inch parchment paper with cooking spray. Then place the parchment paper on top of the muffin tin and place a large scoop of biscuit batter on each of the parchment papers. The batter and the paper will fall to the bottom of each cup.

Now whisk the confectioners' sugar and egg whites together and set aside.

Place the biscuits in the oven and bake for 20 minutes. Remove from the oven and brush each biscuit with the confectioners' sugar mixture. Place back in the oven and bake for 5 more minutes.

Poke a toothpick into the center of the biscuit and if it comes out clean it is done. If not, then bake for an additional 5 minutes. Remove and set aside to cool.

To prepare the lemon curd, whisk together the lemon juice, zest, granulated sugar, and eggs in a heavy saucepan. Stir in the butter and cook over low heat, stirring frequently. After about 5 to 6 minutes, the curd will become thick and stick to the whisk. Remove from heat, transfer curd to a bowl, wrap with plastic wrap, and chill in the refrigerator until cold, about 1 hour.

When the biscuits are cool and the curd is ready, use the end of a wooden spoon to bore a hole in the top of the biscuit about ¼ inch in diameter. Spoon some of the curd into each biscuit until the hole is full. Top with a few blueberries and a mint leaf and serve.

Berry Berry Berry

My mother is a huge inspiration in my life. From important day-to-day life lessons to anything epicurean, she and I are on the phone almost daily chatting about all sorts of things. On a visit to Guerneville she took a little tumble and ended up staying much longer than the planned weekend visit to recover. So we collaborated on a few recipes, and this is one that really stood out for her and many of our loyal biscuit customers. We call it the Berry Berry Berry, because it quite literally has three types of berries buried inside. This combination of blueberries, blackberries, and raspberries is reminiscent of a mixed berry pie, and the addition of a brown sugar glaze on top makes this creation even more irresistible.

Makes 6 biscuits

2 cups self-rising flour

½ teaspoon kosher salt

¼ cup granulated sugar

¼ cup shortening

1 cup buttermilk

⅔ cup heavy cream

¼ cup each fresh blueberries, blackberries, and raspberries, coarsely chopped

For the brown sugar glaze:

½ cup light brown sugar

¼ cup (½ stick) butter, at room temperature

1 egg

1 teaspoon vanilla extract

1 teaspoon ground cinnamon

¼ teaspoon kosher salt

Preheat the oven to 400°F.

Place the flour, salt, granulated sugar, and shortening in a large bowl. Using your hands, blend the ingredients until the shortening is well combined and the mixture looks like small peas.

Add the buttermilk and cream to the biscuit mix and stir until well combined. Now fold in the berries. Set aside and prepare the brown sugar glaze.

Combine all the ingredients for the glaze in a bowl, mix until well combined, and set aside.

Spray a 6-cup jumbo muffin tin and six pieces of 5 x 5-inch parchment paper with cooking spray. Then place the parchment paper on top of the muffin tin and place a large scoop of biscuit batter on each of the parchment papers. The batter and the paper will fall to the bottom of each cup.

Place in the oven and bake for 15 minutes. Brush the top of the biscuits with the brown sugar glaze and bake for another 5 minutes. Poke a toothpick into the center of a biscuit and if it comes out clean it is done. If not, then bake for up to 5 additional minutes. Let cool for 15 to 20 minutes in the pan.

Apple Pie Biscuit

Nothing says nostalgia like a piece of apple pie. At Big Bottom Market, our team combined apple pie with our biscuits to create a "handheld" version of the classic apple pie. Cooking the apples with butter and cinnamon before folding into the batter really helps to bring out the apple pie flavors. And the brown sugar glaze on top tickles the taste buds and will leave you wanting to gobble up one (or two) more. This biscuit is even better when served with a scoop of your favorite vanilla ice cream!

Makes 6 biscuits

2 cups self-rising flour

½ teaspoon kosher salt

¼ cup plus 2 tablespoons granulated sugar

¼ cup shortening

1 cup buttermilk

⅔ cup heavy cream

2 tablespoons butter

1 Granny Smith apple, peeled, cored, and cut into bite-size pieces

½ teaspoon cinnamon

For the crumble:

1 cup all-purpose flour

½ cup light brown sugar

¼ cup (½ stick) butter, at room temperature

1 teaspoon vanilla extract

1 teaspoon ground cinnamon

¼ teaspoon kosher salt

Preheat the oven to 400°F.

Place the flour, salt, ¼ cup granulated sugar, and shortening in a large bowl. Using your hands, blend the ingredients until the shortening is well combined and the mixture looks like small peas.

Add the buttermilk and cream to the biscuit mix and stir until well combined. Set aside.

Prepare the apple pie filling and crumble: In a medium-size saucepan over medium heat melt the butter and then add in the apples, 2 tablespoons of the sugar, and the cinnamon. Let it simmer on low for 3 minutes, until the sugar dissolves and the apples soften slightly. Set aside to cool for 5 minutes.

While the filling is cooling, combine all of the ingredients for the crumble in a bowl, mix until well combined, and set aside.

Fold the apple pie filling into the biscuit dough and set aside. Spray a 6-cup jumbo muffin tin and six pieces of 5 x 5-inch parchment paper with cooking spray. Then place the parchment paper on top of the muffin tin and place a large scoop of biscuit batter on each of the parchment papers. The batter and the paper will fall to the bottom of each cup.

Sprinkle each biscuit with some of the crumb topping, place in the oven, and bake for 20 minutes. Poke a toothpick into the center of the biscuit and if it comes out clean it is done. If not, then bake for up to 5 additional minutes. Let cool for 15 to 20 minutes.

Choco Coco Almond

This is an Arturo biscuit. Arturo has been working at the Market since the very beginning and can run every inch of the place. He is an expert line cook, very creative baker, and a really good guy. We proudly display his unique concoctions, and this one is no exception. Any lover of chocolate, coconut, and almonds will want to gobble this up. The nutty goodness of the almond paired with sweet and chewy coconut and the richness of chocolate makes for a delightful treat.

Makes 6 biscuits

2 cups self-rising flour

½ teaspoon kosher salt

¼ cup granulated sugar

¼ cup shortening

1 cup buttermilk

⅔ cup heavy cream

¼ cup semisweet chocolate chips

¼ cup chopped roasted almonds

¼ cup dried and shredded coconut

Creamy chocolate topping, for drizzling (page 53)

Preheat the oven to 400°F.

Place the flour, salt, granulated sugar, and shortening in a large bowl. Using your hands, blend the ingredients until the shortening is well combined and the mixture looks like small peas.

Add the buttermilk, cream, chocolate, almonds, and coconut to the biscuit mix and stir until well combined.

Spray a 6-cup jumbo muffin tin and six pieces of 5 x 5-inch parchment paper with cooking spray. Then place the parchment paper on top of the muffin tin and place a large scoop of biscuit batter on each of the parchment papers. The batter and the paper will fall to the bottom of each cup.

Bake for 20 minutes. Poke a toothpick into the center of the biscuit and if it comes out clean it is done. If not, then bake for up to 5 additional minutes. Let cool for 15 to 20 minutes.

While the biscuits are cooling, prepare the creamy chocolate topping. Drizzle it on top of the biscuits, and they are ready to be served.

Biscuit BLT

Who doesn't love a BLT? Wait, let me rephrase that: who doesn't love a *biscuit* BLT? If you've never had a Biscuit BLT before, this one is a must-try. We serve this as a special at the market during heirloom tomato season. In fact, more and more grocery stores are bringing in ripe and delicious tomatoes all year long, so why wait until summertime for what you can have today?

Makes 9 biscuit BLT sandwiches

9 Original Big Bottom Biscuits (page 20)

1½ cups Lemon Garlic Aioli (page 99)

9 pieces romaine lettuce, washed

3 to 4 tomatoes, sliced (I prefer heirlooms for this recipe)

18 to 20 pieces of cooked bacon

Start by splitting the nine biscuits in half and slathering aioli on both sides of the biscuit. Now build your sandwich starting with lettuce on the bottom, followed by a slice of tomato (or two), and then two pieces of bacon. Serve. It's that easy!

VARIATION: Try this with Jalapeño Jam (page 97)—the heat from the peppers really adds a zesty kick to this sandwich! We finish the top of each biscuit with a combination of aioli and a little Jalapeño Jam for those who like it a little spicy.

NOTE: If you can't find heirloom tomatoes and your only choice is beefsteak or plum tomatoes, you can slow roast these to create what I call tomato candy. Preheat the oven to 250°F. Coat the bottom of a cookie sheet with extra-virgin olive oil. Cut thick slices of three to four beefsteak or plum tomatoes and space evenly on the cookie sheet. Roast for about 45 minutes to 1 hour. Check frequently to ensure that the slices are slowly roasting and not burning. The result is an amazingly sweet stand-in for the heirloom.

BUTT

JAMS, S

AND

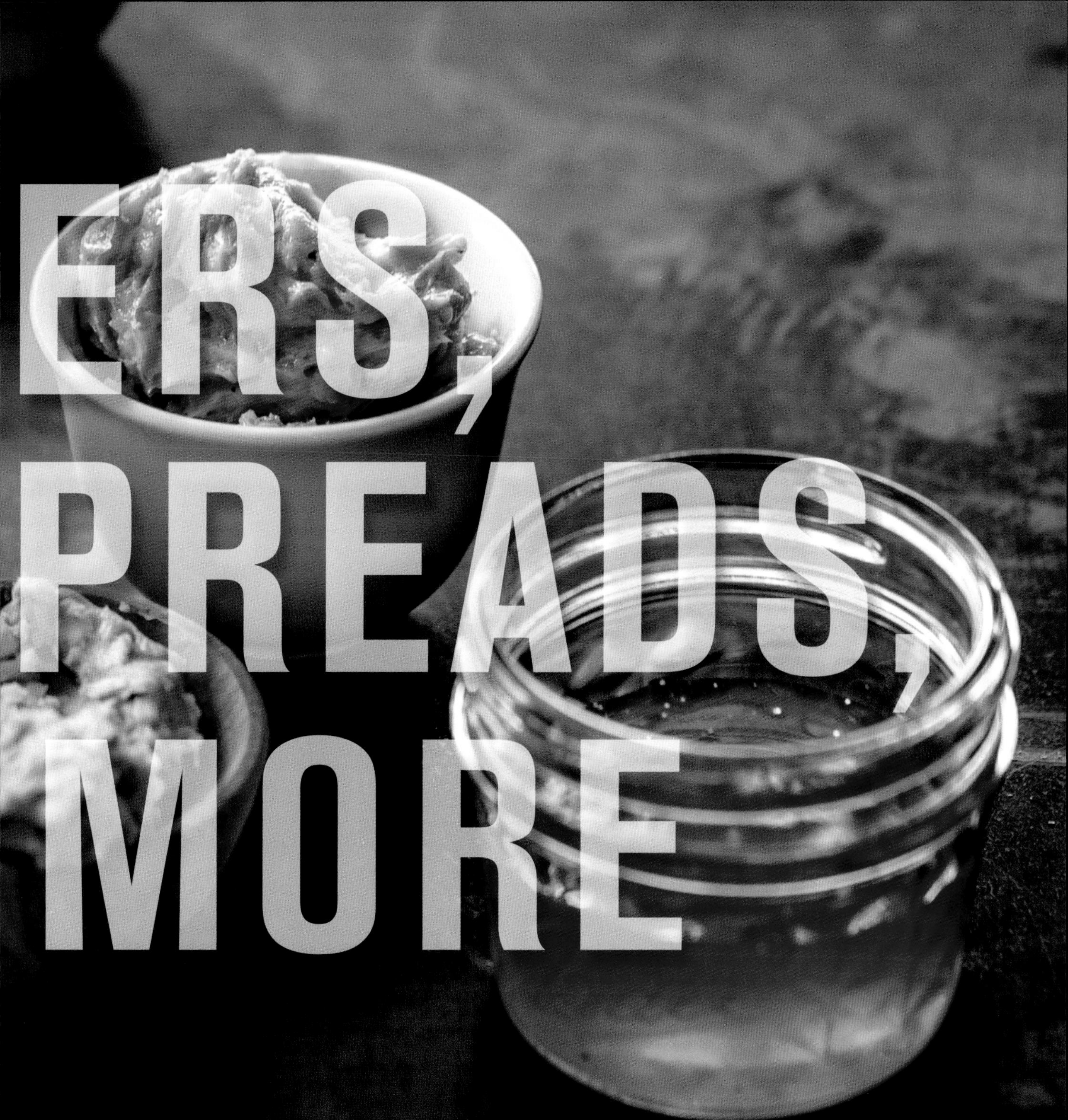

ERS, PREADS, MORE

Ask any biscuit lover: a warm biscuit is best with butter and jam. As the butter slowly melts on top of the biscuit, it mingles with the jam and adds a depth of flavor that literally engulfs your taste buds in sweetness.

In our constant effort to elevate the biscuit beyond the traditional, we've come up with dozens of tasty butters, jams, and spreads. The recipes in this chapter give you everything you need to test and taste some of what we make in the Market.

In most cases the following recipes can be served as an accompaniment to the biscuit, either to top a biscuit or spread on a sliced biscuit. We love unique combinations—like sweet jams with cheese on a Mini Biscuit (page 22) as an appetizer. The savory butters go well on top of meats, especially the Blue Cheese and Honey Butter (we especially like this one on a rib eye steak). They can also be paired with jams or served just as they are.

Finally, we've outlined how to set up your own biscuit bar (page 140) to help take your upcoming brunch to the next level.

A NOTE ON COMPOUND BUTTERS

Compound butters are simply a mix of butter and other ingredients. They are primarily used to enhance a finished dish, but at the market we serve them with our famous biscuit. All of the recipes here can be refrigerated for about 5 days or frozen for up to 6 months. The following pages include a few of our favorites. If you have an interesting combination, hop on to our Facebook page and share it with us. We love it when our customers share their creative ideas.

Honey Butter

Makes about 16 pats of butter

1 cup (2 sticks) unsalted butter
½ teaspoon kosher salt
¼ cup Big Bottom Market Orange Blossom Honey or your favorite local honey

Cut the butter into chunks.

Place the butter into a standing mixer with a whisk attachment and beat at low speed. Add the salt and honey and beat until well combined, 1 to 2 minutes. Remove the butter from the bowl and spoon onto parchment paper or plastic wrap. Roll into a log and refrigerate for 2 hours or until the butter can be sliced into pieces. When ready, slice into ¼-inch pieces.

Honey and Blue Cheese Butter

Makes about 16 pats of butter

1 cup (2 sticks) unsalted butter
¼ cup Big Bottom Market Orange Blossom Honey or your favorite local honey
⅔ cup crumbled blue cheese
½ teaspoon kosher salt

Cut the butter into chunks.

Place the butter into a standing mixer with a whisk attachment and beat at low speed. Add the honey, cheese, and salt and beat until well combined, 1 to 2 minutes. Remove the butter from the bowl and spoon onto parchment paper or plastic wrap. Roll into a log and refrigerate for 2 hours or until the butter can be sliced into pieces. When ready, slice into ¼-inch pieces.

This pairs very nicely with a glass of dry white wine.

Honey, Roasted Carrot, and Turmeric Butter

Makes about 16 pats of butter

1 cup (2 sticks) unsalted butter

1 large carrot

¼ cup Big Bottom Market Orange Blossom Honey or your favorite local honey

2 teaspoons turmeric powder

½ teaspoon kosher salt

Cut the butter into chunks.

Roast the carrot on a cookie sheet in the oven for 25 to 30 minutes at 350°F, until very soft. Let cool completely, then mash the carrot with a fork until smooth.

Place the butter into a standing mixer with a whisk attachment and beat at low speed. Add the carrot, honey, turmeric, and salt and beat until well combined, 1 to 2 minutes. Remove the butter from the bowl and spoon onto parchment paper or plastic wrap. Roll into a log and refrigerate for 2 hours or until the butter can be sliced into pieces. When ready, slice into ¼-inch pieces.

NOTE: Beyond the biscuit, this compound butter is lovely atop a piece of grilled fish. I prefer halibut, swordfish, or tilapia for the firm texture. These grill up easily and with a pat of this special compound butter along with a dash of salt and freshly ground black pepper, your palate will thank you. Don't forget to serve this fish with a biscuit for your starch and a lovely mixed green salad with Champagne Vinaigrette (page 84).

Honey Avocado Butter

Makes about 20 pats of butter

1 cup (2 sticks) unsalted butter

¼ cup Big Bottom Market Orange Blossom Honey or your favorite local honey

1 ripe avocado

2 tablespoons fresh lemon juice

½ teaspoon kosher salt

Cut the butter into chunks.

Place the butter into a standing mixer with a whisk attachment and beat at low speed. Add the honey, avocado, lemon juice (which will keep the avocado from browning), and salt and beat until well combined, 1 to 2 minutes. Remove the butter from the bowl and spoon onto parchment paper or plastic wrap. Roll into a log and refrigerate for 2 hours or until the butter can be sliced into pieces. When ready, slice into ¼-inch pieces.

A Note about Honey

Two of my best gal pals, Heidi and Deneene, laugh at me because of my fascination with honey—Big Bottom Market partners with apiaries all over California. Some of these hives live among orange groves, vineyards, and a host of flora that all help to create sweet and delicious honey. Needless to say, these bees are well taken care of and the flavor of our honey always matches the terroir and environment where these little honey makers thrive.

Much of the honey we use is pure and unpasteurized, which means that it can crystallize when it sits for a long time unused (if you use as much honey as we do, this likely won't happen). If it does happen, don't fret—pure, raw, unheated honey has a natural tendency to crystallize over time with no effect to the honey other than color and texture. Place the jar, with lid tightly fastened, in a pot of warm water on the stove (don't worry, it won't hurt the honey at all), set the heat to medium-low, and stir until the crystals dissolve. You can also place the honey in a pot of hot water and leave it alone until it liquefies. For a quick fix, you can heat the jar in the microwave for 30 seconds, stir well, allow to cool for 20 seconds, and then heat again for 30 seconds more.

Whipped Mascarpone and Honey

This is a big seller at the Market and is an easy one to prepare. During the photo shoot for this book, Kelly, our amazing photographer, asked us as she was shooting this tasty dish, "Is this for breakfast, dessert, or both?" I had never really thought about it, but quickly replied, "both." Whether in the morning or after a hearty meal, this dish always pleases the palate no matter the time of day.

Makes 6 biscuits

6 Original Big Bottom Biscuits (page 20)
3 cups Mascarpone cheese
⅓ cup honey, plus additional for drizzling (you can use a honey bear or plastic squeeze bottle to make drizzling easier)
6 fresh mint leaves

Place the Mascarpone cheese into a bowl and fold in the honey using a spatula.

Slice the biscuits in half and put the bottom of the biscuit in the bowl. Scoop about ½ cup mascarpone onto each biscuit and top with the other half of the biscuit. Drizzle with additional honey, garnish the top with a mint leaf, and serve. It will be deliciously messy!

Champagne Vinaigrette

Many of our dishes at the Market come with mixed greens with Champagne Vinaigrette. This is pretty easy to make and stores in the refrigerator for up to 2 weeks.

Makes 3 cups

1 cup Champagne vinegar
½ tablespoon chopped garlic
1½ teaspoons kosher salt
1½ cups extra-virgin olive oil
½ cup canola oil

Combine all the ingredients except the oils into a blender or food processor. (Your blender or food processor should be fitted with a top that will allow you to pour the oil into the mixture as it is blending.) Combine the oils into a measuring cup with a pour spout. Once the top is tightly fitted, turn it on low and start to slowly pour the oils into the blender or processor. Once the oils are fully incorporated, place the vinaigrette into an airtight container and store in the refrigerator for up to 2 weeks. Serve atop mixed greens and on the side of any delicious biscuit sandwich and other savory dishes.

Cumin Vinaigrette

Not everybody loves gluten, and while we have tested a bunch of flours in an effort to make a gluten-free biscuit worthy of the Market, our team has yet to find the right one. For those with a gluten intolerance we give our guests the ability to transform their favorite biscuit sandwiches into salads. One of the most popular renditions of this is our Colonel Armstrong Curry Chicken Salad (page 138). For this dish, we serve it on greens dressed with our homemade Cumin Vinaigrette. This vinaigrette is delicious and will store in the refrigerator for up to 2 weeks.

Makes 3 cups

1 cup apple cider vinegar
2½ tablespoons ground cumin
2½ tablespoons honey
2½ tablespoons Dijon mustard
1½ teaspoons kosher salt
1½ cups extra-virgin olive oil
½ cup canola oil

Combine all the ingredients except the oils into an immersion blender or food processor. (Your blender or food processor should be fitted with a top that will allow you to pour the oil into the mixture as it is blending.) Combine the oils in a measuring cup with a pour spout. Once the top is tightly fitted, turn it on low and start to slowly pour the oils into the blender or processor. Once the oils are fully incorporated, place the vinaigrette into an airtight container and store in the refrigerator for up to 2 weeks. Serve atop mixed greens topped with curry chicken salad.

Mushroom Duxelles

My good friends Lee and Betsy Deiseroth are the owners of The Fluted Mushroom in Pittsburgh, PA, where I grew up. While I was in college I worked there and spent my weekends prepping food, helping set up for parties, and also serving. I credit the team at The Fluted Mushroom for teaching me excellent knife skills, kitchen prep, and how to put together a gorgeous crudités platter. The team of chefs also taught me how to make Mushroom Duxelles. I love this recipe so much that it has become a staple in my kitchen and especially at cocktail parties. It is typically served on a crusty baguette, but goes oh so well as a spread on the Original Big Bottom Biscuit (page 20) or Mini Biscuit (page 22).

Makes 2 cups

2 tablespoons extra-virgin olive oil

2 large shallots, chopped

1 tablespoon minced garlic

8 cups cremini mushrooms

2 cups dry red wine

2 tablespoons chopped parsley

2 teaspoons fresh thyme

3 teaspoons kosher salt, plus more to taste

3 teaspoons freshly ground black pepper, plus more to taste

Mini Biscuits (page 22), for serving

Cover the bottom of a large sauté pan on medium heat with olive oil. Add in the shallots and garlic and sauté for 2 minutes. Add in the mushrooms and wine and turn the heat up to high. As the wine begins to boil, add the parsley, thyme, salt, and pepper. Let the wine cook down all the way and remove the pan from the stove.

Transfer the ingredients to a food processor and pulverize into a spread. Remove from the processor and add additional salt and pepper to taste. Serve as a spread next to a plate of biscuits or make canapés with the Mini Biscuits. This will keep for up to 1 week in the refrigerator.

Spinach Artichoke Spread

We cannot keep this one in our grab-and-go. Every time we make a batch and package it up, our guests gobble it up. This version in particular has a unique flavor profile, because we use our house-made Lemon Garlic Aioli.

Makes about 4 to 5 cups

3 cups canned artichokes, drained

⅓ cup Lemon Garlic Aioli (page 99)

1 cup cooked spinach, with excess water squeezed out

1 teaspoon kosher salt

½ cup grated Parmesan

1 tablespoon honey

Mini Biscuits (page 22), for serving

This recipe is pretty simple. Place all of the ingredients except Mini Biscuits into a food processor and blend until smooth. Remove from the bowl (use a spatula for this part so you get each and every bit out) and serve atop Mini Biscuits as an appetizer. This dip will store in the fridge for about a week.

Sweet and Savory Jams

Biscuit + Butter + Homemade Jam = Delicious. While math has never been my strong suit, this is one equation that comes easily to me. The savory and sweet jams collected here are easy to make and don't require pectin, a gelatinous substance that is used as a thickening agent. The process of cooking the fruits, sugar, and other ingredients down, along with cooling in the refrigerator, naturally thickens these tasty jams.

Rosemary Orange Marmalade

Makes 2 cups

This one takes me back. My mother has always loved the combination of orange marmalade with ham on a crusty French roll, and to be honest, I do too. I decided to come up with my own version of marmalade with a twist. Rosemary is abundant in Sonoma County and pairs well with the sweetness of marmalade. You can serve this one on its own or top a biscuit bottom with some honey ham and a dollop of Rosemary Orange Marmalade for a remarkable sandwich. Try to find organic, unwaxed fruit for making the marmalade.

3 oranges
⅓ cup dry white wine
1 sprig fresh rosemary, about 3 inches long
1½ cups granulated sugar

Wash oranges with peel on, cut in half, and remove any visible seeds. Pulse the oranges in a food processor until you have a finely chopped pulp.

Place the orange pulp, white wine, rosemary, and sugar into a sauté pan over medium heat. Stir continuously and cook until the jam is thickened, 15 to 20 minutes.

Remove from the heat and transfer the jam to a large airtight jar or container. Cool in the refrigerator for at least 2 hours. As the jam cools it will thicken even more. The jam will last in the refrigerator for up to 10 days.

Blueberry Thyme

Thyme is subtle, and with its dry aroma and slightly minty flavor, it pairs well with the mellow sweetness of the blueberry. It's been said that thyme was used in the 1800s as a cure for a hangover, so maybe save this one for the morning after. Your headache may not go away, but couple this jam with a biscuit and your tummy will thank you.

Makes 2 cups

5 cups fresh or frozen blueberries
1½ cups granulated sugar
2 tablespoons fresh thyme

Clean the blueberries and place them into a sauté pan over medium heat with the sugar and thyme. Stir continuously and cook until the jam is thickened, 15 to 20 minutes. Remove from the heat and place the jam into a food processor. Pulse a few times until blueberries are pulverized. Transfer the jam to a large airtight jar or container. Cool in the refrigerator for at least 2 hours. As the jam cools it will thicken even more. The jam will last in the refrigerator for up to 10 days.

Shallot Jam

We typically use this jam on sandwiches, but it also tastes great slathered on a biscuit. If you want to kick things up a notch, pair this shallot jam with goat cheese or feta—the jam and cheese combination is a great option for the Mini Biscuit (page 22) and will work perfectly as a canapé for your next event.

Makes 2 cups

4 cups shallots, skins removed

1 tablespoon extra-virgin olive oil

1 tablespoon sherry vinegar

2 cups dry red wine

¼ cup honey

½ cup granulated sugar

Place the shallots in a food processor and pulse until coarsely chopped.

Place the olive oil and shallots into a sauté pan and cook over medium heat, stirring constantly until translucent, 2 to 3 minutes. Add in the vinegar, wine, honey, and sugar. Continue to cook, stirring continuously until the jam is thickened, 15 to 20 minutes. Remove from the heat and store in a large airtight jar or container. Cool in the refrigerator for at least 2 hours. As the jam cools it will thicken even more. The jam will last in the refrigerator for up to 10 days.

Simple Strawberry Jam

My mother made strawberry jam in the summertime when they were at their sweetest. I was always fascinated by the process and the amount that she would make. It lasted in the freezer all year long and I couldn't bear using store-bought jam with access to the deliciousness of homemade.

Makes 2 cups

4 cups fresh strawberries
½ cup granulated sugar
½ cup honey
⅓ cup fresh lemon juice

Process the strawberries in a food processor until coarsely chopped.

Then put the chopped strawberries in a sauté pan over medium heat and add in the sugar, honey, and lemon juice. Stir continuously and cook until the jam is thickened, 15 to 20 minutes.

Remove from the heat and store in a large airtight jar or container. Cool in the refrigerator for at least 2 hours. As the jam cools it will thicken even more. The jam will last in the refrigerator for up to 10 days.

NOTE: For this recipe I like to buy fresh strawberries and freeze them before chopping them up in the food processor. They should chop easily and evenly. If you really want to be a purist you can chop them by hand, but the freezer to processor method, in my opinion, is easier. You can also use store-bought frozen berries, but make sure that when you buy frozen no sugar has been added. If all you have are frozen berries with sugar already added, be sure to back down on the amount of sugar you use in this recipe by 1 cup. You can always taste when done and add in more sugar if you want your jam to be sweeter.

Red Bell Pepper Jam

When you make this jam your kitchen will be filled with fabulous aromas. The combination of the sweet red bell peppers, honey and sugar, red pepper flakes, and sherry vinegar really gives this simple jam a balanced and remarkable flavor. There is a lot of water in bell peppers, so this one has to cook down a little longer. The wait, however, is well worth it.

Makes 2½ cups

6 red bell peppers, washed and seeded

1 tablespoon extra-virgin olive oil

1 teaspoon crushed red pepper flakes (or more if you want it really spicy)

¼ cup honey

1¾ cups granulated sugar

¾ cup sherry vinegar

2 tablespoons kosher salt

Place the peppers in a food processor and pulse until coarsely chopped. Make sure you don't have any large pieces left. You can always pull bigger stragglers out and chop them with a knife so they are uniform with the rest of the peppers. Then place the peppers in a sieve or on a piece of cheesecloth and press out the liquid.

Heat the olive oil in a medium saucepan and add in the peppers, pepper flakes, honey, sugar, vinegar, and salt. Cook down, stirring regularly for 25 to 30 minutes. It will be time to take the jam off the heat when the bubbling reduces and the liquid has reduced considerably and is almost gone.

Transfer into a large airtight jar or container with a lid and cool in the refrigerator for at least 2 hours. As the jam cools it will thicken even more. The jam will last in the refrigerator for up to 10 days.

VARIATION: This jam is amazing when served on a biscuit with cheese. Follow the recipe for Mini Biscuits (page 22) to make a fabulous canapé with Red Bell Pepper Jam and goat cheese (or Brie or white Cheddar), and serve with your favorite sparkling wine.

Jalapeño Jam

Our most popular sandwich at the Market is the Parson Jones—roasted turkey, Havarti cheese, arugula, aioli, and Jalapeño Jam on a French roll. Sometimes I replace the French roll with a warm biscuit. The spicy jam and aioli are a perfect marriage on the warm biscuit along with all of the other fantastic ingredients. Keep in mind the more seeds you add in from the jalapeño, the spicier the jam will be. If you're not a fan of super spicy, only use a small amount of seeds.

Makes 2 cups

4 green bell peppers, washed and seeded
1 jalapeño, including half of the seeds
2 cups dry white wine
½ cup granulated sugar
¼ cup honey

Place the green peppers and jalapeño with seeds into a food processor and pulse until finely chopped. Transfer into a medium sauté pan with the remaining ingredients and cook over medium heat, stirring continuously until the liquids have dissipated and the jam is thickened, 25 to 30 minutes. Remove from the heat, place into a container with a lid and cool in the refrigerator for at least 2 hours. As the jam cools it will thicken even more. The jam will last in the refrigerator for up to 10 days.

Lemon Garlic Aioli

This Lemon Garlic Aioli is the basis for many of our sandwiches, biscuits, and salads at the market. We've made it hundreds of times and have mastered the process. For this aioli, we use a combination of canola oil and extra-virgin olive oil, because the canola tones down the grassiness of the olive oil. Slather this on sandwiches and biscuits, of course, or use it for the base of a chicken or egg salad. This aioli is versatile and the options are endless.

Makes 4 cups

1 to 2 garlic cloves
4 large eggs
½ tablespoon fresh lemon juice
1 teaspoon kosher salt
1½ cups canola oil
2½ cups extra-virgin olive oil

Place the garlic, eggs, lemon juice, and salt into a blender or food processor. Your blender or food processor should be fitted with a top that will allow you to slowly pour the oil into the mixture as it is blending. Combine the oils into a measuring cup with a pour spout.

Once the top is tightly fitted, start the blender or processor and begin to very slowly pour the oils into the blender or processor through the feed tube or spout. You'll see the aioli begin to form. Once you've poured all of the oil into the bowl and the aioli is thick, turn off the processor and transfer to an airtight container. You can keep the aioli in the fridge for up to 2 weeks.

VARIATION: This aioli is super versatile and you can use a number of ingredients to make it even more flavorful than it already is. My good friend and amazing chef, Jenn Garagliano, tasted this and immediately mused, "This would be so good when mixed with the Sun-Dried Tomato Spread and slathered on a sandwich." Combine ¼ cup of the Sun-Dried Tomato Spread (page 103) with ½ cup aioli and whisk until smooth. You can also use mayonnaise.

Pimiento Cheese Spread

Simply easy to prepare, this rich spread goes well with the Original Big Bottom Biscuit (page 20) and is especially appropriate as a canapé with the Mini Biscuit (page 22). Whenever we prepare our version of Pimiento Cheese Spread it flies off the shelves. If you want to make your life really easy head to your local grocery store or gourmet shop and buy grated cheese at a level of sharpness that suits your palate.

Makes 2 cups

2 cups shredded yellow cheddar cheese

4 ounces cream cheese, at room temperature

2 ounces jarred pimientos

3 tablespoons Jalapeño Jam (page 97)

2 tablespoons Greek yogurt

¼ teaspoon kosher salt

¼ teaspoon freshly ground black pepper

Mini Biscuits (page 22), for serving

Place all the ingredients in a standing mixer fitted with a paddle. Mix the ingredients on medium speed until smooth and spreadable, about 1½ minutes.

Transfer the pimiento cheese to a bowl or plastic container, cover, and store in the refrigerator for up to 1 week.

Lentil Walnut Paté

The word *paté* likely makes you think of meat, specifically liver. This paté, however, is a veggie version and a wonderful accompaniment when paired with the Mini Biscuit (page 22). We serve this on our Mezze platter at the Market, but it also works well as a savory if you decide to host a biscuit bar party (page 140). While walnuts are the nut of choice in this recipe, you could also use almonds, pine nuts, or no nuts at all.

Makes 2½ cups

2 cups cooked black lentils

1 cup toasted walnuts

1 tablespoon ground cinnamon

1 tablespoon ground cumin

1 tablespoon cayenne pepper

1 tablespoon paprika

¼ cup fresh lemon juice (1 lemon)

½ cup extra-virgin olive oil

Salt and freshly ground black pepper, to taste

Mini Biscuits (page 22), for serving

Combine all the ingredients except the oil, salt, pepper, and Mini Biscuits into a blender or food processor. Your blender or food processor should be fitted with a top that will allow you to slowly pour the oil into the mixture as it is blending.

Place the oil into a measuring cup with a pour spout. Once the top is tightly fitted, start to slowly pour the oils into the blender or processor and turn it on low. Once the oils are fully incorporated, add salt and pepper to taste. Transfer the paté to an airtight container and store in the refrigerator for up to 5 days.

VARIATION: You don't have to use walnuts in this recipe. I love substituting pine nuts for walnuts. Toast the nuts for about 2 minutes in a small sauté pan over medium heat while stirring constantly. Add this into the blender or food processor with the rest of the ingredients.

Sun-Dried Tomato Spread

I absolutely love this spread. It not only has a quick preparation process, but it is also very tasty. We use Sriracha to spice this up, but you can substitute with your favorite hot sauce or crushed red pepper to give it the zing you desire. Spread this on Mini Biscuits (page 22), top with your favorite blue cheese, and serve to your guests—whose mouths will likely water as they beg for more. Once arranged on the platter, you can also chiffonade some additional basil leaves and sprinkle on top to garnish.

Makes 2½ cups

1 (6-ounce) can tomato paste

2 (7-ounce) jars sun-dried tomatoes, oil drained and chopped

2 tablespoons honey

5 fresh basil leaves

2 teaspoons garlic cloves

Zest from ½ lemon (about 1 teaspoon)

1 tablespoon fresh lemon juice

4 ounces cream cheese, at room temperature

1 teaspoon Sriracha (you can add more if you want a spicier spread)

½ teaspoon kosher salt

Mini Biscuits (page 22), for serving

Place all of the ingredients except the biscuits into a medium-size mixing bowl. Using a spatula fold the ingredients together until well blended. Serve immediately on Mini Biscuits as a canapé or transfer to an airtight container. This will store in the refrigerator for 1 week.

Our team is constantly testing and tasting in an effort to not only offer alternatives to how we make and use the biscuit but also to elevate it beyond the traditional breakfast item. So we've come up with delicious dishes that transcend epicurean dimensions. The recipes are inspired by family favorites, worldwide travels, and some of our most loyal customers. The Creamy Shrimp Soup (page 112) is a nod to a delicious and regional recipe that my cousin Lou Lou and her husband PJ made at their restaurant in Annapolis, Maryland. Ribollita (page 118) is a classic Italian dish that was made by our good friend Randall for a private dinner at the Market and one that perfectly pairs with the biscuit. The Mediterranean Spiced Chicken with Tzatziki (page 133) is inspired by one of my favorite foodie families and the time I spent cooking in the kitchen with the matriarch and good friend Janet. We've even provided all of the details you need to create your very own biscuit bar. All of the recipes in this section will help you expand how to serve biscuits beyond breakfast and make your next savory meal one to remember.

Biscuits with Veggie Gravy

What is a biscuit without a topping of sinfully delicious gravy? We use this vegetarian recipe as a base. While it is wonderful on its own, we have also included a few variations at the end of this recipe that will make your mouth water. This gravy recipe also tastes amazing atop fried chicken or chicken fried steak. Especially when served with a biscuit on the side, of course.

Makes 6 servings

¼ cup (½ stick) unsalted butter

3 cups all-purpose flour

3 cups heavy cream

2½ teaspoons ground nutmeg

¾ teaspoon cayenne pepper

⅔ cup fresh thyme (you can substitute 3 tablespoons dried, but fresh is always better)

4½ teaspoons dried mustard

Kosher salt, to taste

6 biscuits (page 20), for serving

In a saucepan, melt the butter and add in the flour. Whisk the butter and flour together until a thick paste forms (this is called a roux). Continue to stir for 3 to 5 minutes and then add in the cream, nutmeg, cayenne pepper, thyme, and mustard. Continue stirring until ingredients are well incorporated and the cream begins to thicken into a gravy. Add a little bit of salt to taste, and if your palate calls for additional, then add a little more.

Place each biscuit in a shallow bowl or on a plate. Ladle the gravy on top. Serve hot.

VARIATIONS: You can make this recipe spicier by adding in a little more cayenne pepper. It's also great with the addition of chopped tomatoes (½ to ¾ cup) for a simple tomato gravy. If you are feeling especially hungry and don't mind a few more calories, you can add in cooked sausage or bacon, or top the biscuit with an egg—the options are endless so use your imagination and be creative.

Biscuit Veggie Tikka Masala

Tikka Masala is one of my favorite Indian dishes. The combination of spices in this dish liven up the palate and can stay with you for hours following a meal. We love the combination of our sweet biscuit with this amazing rendition of a traditional Indian classic. According to our former executive chef and good friend, Tricia Brown, this dish pairs very nicely with an aromatic white wine like Gewürztraminer or a juicy Zinfandel.

Makes 9 servings

6 garlic cloves, diced

4 teaspoons chopped fresh ginger

4 teaspoons ground turmeric

2 teaspoons cardamom

2 teaspoons garam masala

2 teaspoons coriander

2 teaspoons ground cumin

1 tablespoon kosher salt

2 cups Greek yogurt

1 (12-ounce) can chickpeas, drained and rinsed

2 cups chopped carrots

2 cups chopped cauliflower

3 tablespoons ghee (clarified butter that can be purchased at a gourmet or Indian grocery store) or vegetable oil

1 small onion, thinly sliced

¼ cup tomato paste

2 dried Pasilla (or chile negro) chile peppers, or ½ teaspoon crushed red pepper flakes

1 (28-ounce) can whole peeled tomatoes

4 cups heavy cream

2 tablespoons Big Bottom Market Orange Blossom Honey or your favorite local honey, plus extra for garnish

9 Original Big Bottom Biscuits (page 20)

½ cup pickled onions, for garnish (page 34)

½ cup chopped fresh cilantro, for garnish

Zest from 1 lime (about 1 teaspoon), for garnish

Combine the garlic, ginger, turmeric, cardamom, garam masala, coriander, cumin, and salt in a small bowl.

Whisk the yogurt and half of the spice mixture together in a medium bowl and then add in the chickpeas, carrots, and cauliflower. Set the remaining spice mixture aside. Mix the veggies well, being sure to coat the veggies with the yogurt spice mixture. Cover and chill for at least 1 hour.

Heat the ghee in a large pot over medium heat. Add the onion and cook until translucent, 3 to 5 minutes. Add the reserved spice mixture, tomato paste, and chiles and cook, stirring often, until the bottom of the pot begins to brown, 3 to 5 minutes.

Purée the tomatoes in a blender and add to the pot. As the tomatoes begin to boil, reduce the heat and simmer, stirring often and scraping up browned bits from the bottom of the pot. The sauce will begin to thicken in 8 to 10 minutes. Add the cream and honey and simmer, stirring occasionally, until the sauce thickens, 30 to 40 minutes.

Preheat the oven to 350°F. Transfer the veggie-yogurt mixture to a large cookie sheet. Cover the entire sheet with the mixture. Cook the veggies until they begin to char, about 10 minutes. Turn the pan around in the oven halfway and cook for an additional 10 minutes. Remove from the oven and add to the large pot. Stir well and continue to cook for an additional 30 minutes on medium heat, or until the veggies are cooked through.

To serve, slice a biscuit in half and place the bottom into a bowl. Using a soup spoon, place two scoops of the veggie Masala on top of the biscuit. Top with some pickled onions, a drizzle of honey, and some cilantro. Zest some lime on top and serve.

Creamy Shrimp Soup

Back in the day (way, way back) my cousin Lou Lou (may she rest in peace) and her husband PJ owned a fabulous restaurant on Ritchie Highway in Maryland. Only a few miles from the Bay Bridge and downtown Annapolis, the Oxbow Inn was known for its delicious seafood dishes that were prepared under the guidance of PJ. One of my favorites was a creamy crab soup—Maryland is well known for blue crab, and the Oxbow put the succulent jumbo lump crabmeat to good use. We've opted for shrimp in this recipe, but the flavor profile, highlighted by the sherry, homemade shrimp stock, and cayenne pepper, takes me back to the Oxbow. Thanks to PJ for sharing this with the Market and now the world. Of course, it goes without saying that this soup goes really well with a biscuit on the side to sop up the creamy broth and give it some extra richness.

8 cups whole milk

4 cups heavy cream

4 cups fish stock

1 cup dry sherry

1 tablespoon kosher salt, plus more to taste

1 tablespoon freshly ground black pepper, plus more to taste

2 pounds uncooked shrimp, shelled and deveined

½ cup fresh parsley

6 to 8 Original Big Bottom Biscuits (page 20)

For the roux:

1½ cups (3 sticks) unsalted butter

½ cup all-purpose flour

In a medium stock pot on low heat, combine all the ingredients, except for the shrimp, parsley, and biscuits. Let the contents warm up without getting to a rolling boil.

As the soup base is cooking, make the roux. Melt the butter in a saucepan over medium heat. Add in the flour and stir constantly for 3 to 5 minutes to produce a light roux.

Transfer the roux to the stock pot and continue to cook while whisking the soup for another 3 to 5 minutes. As the mixture starts to thicken, add in the shrimp and parsley. Once the shrimp is pink and cooked through, the soup is ready to be served.

There are two ways to serve this dish. You can serve the biscuits on the side. However, if you really want to make something decadent, then place a biscuit in a medium-size shallow serving bowl and pour the soup right on top. The biscuit will soak up the soup and you'll have a hearty meal that everyone will salivate over.

VARIATION: I like to make a quick shrimp stock and fortify it with 2 tablespoons of vegetable bouillon. Buy a 2-pound bag of uncooked frozen or fresh shrimp with the shell and tail intact. I prefer to buy them already deveined, but if you cannot find the shrimp without the vein you'll have to do it yourself. Peel the shrimp, place the shells in a medium stock pot, and set the shrimp meat aside. Add a carrot, celery stick, half an onion with the skin on, 3 garlic cloves, and 1 tablespoon black peppercorns. Cover with 6 cups of water and let it cook down for 20 to 30 minutes. The essence of the shrimp shells will permeate the water while the veggies and garlic add additional depth of flavor. Strain into a bowl and add in 2 tablespoons of vegetable bouillon. This will take the place of store-bought fish stock.

Market Pulled Pork

With so much prep work to do, Theresa, our amazing cook at the Market, absolutely loves the simplicity of this recipe. Put everything in a Dutch oven and bake. It is literally that easy and the result is truly amazing. Top with your favorite dill or sweet pickle slices or add in some of the leftover sauce before serving. This recipe produces a lot of sauce that melds so beautifully with the drippings from the meat. The recipe explains how to turn this into a sauce that you can use to further season the pulled pork atop a biscuit. Store any leftover sauce in the refrigerator for about a week. Pulled pork has a rich and silky flavor that marries perfectly with the elegance of a fantastic Russian River pinot.

Makes 6 to 8 servings

1 tablespoon coriander

1 tablespoon turmeric

1 tablespoon cumin

2 tablespoons honey, plus more for taste

2 teaspoons dried mustard

2 teaspoons fennel seed

1 tablespoon paprika

1 tablespoon fresh thyme

2 teaspoons kosher salt, plus more to taste

2 teaspoons freshly ground black pepper

2 (28-ounce) cans Italian peeled tomatoes

1 large onion, roughly chopped (about 2½ cups)

2 tablespoons extra-virgin olive oil

2 (12-ounce) cans chicken broth

3 cups dry white wine

3½- to 4-pound bone-in pork shoulder

6 to 8 Original Big Bottom Biscuits (page 20)

Coleslaw (page 35, optional)

Preheat the oven to 250°F.

Stir the coriander, turmeric, cumin, honey, mustard, fennel seed, paprika, thyme, salt, pepper, tomatoes, onion, olive oil, chicken broth, and wine together in a Dutch oven. Add the pork shoulder and turn to coat all over with the liquid. Cover tightly and bake in the oven for 6 to 8 hours, or until the pork shreds easily with a fork. If the pork is not shredding, place back into the oven and cook for an additional 30 minutes to 1 hour. Let cool for 30 to 40 minutes. When cool, remove the pork shoulder, take out the bone, and pull apart with a fork in a large bowl. Fall-apart meat such as pulled pork is achieved because the connective tissue has become soluble with cooking. Too short a cook time will result in tough meat, and nobody likes tough meat.

Use an immersion blender (or regular blender) to purée the remaining sauce in the Dutch oven. Taste and add additional salt and honey as desired.

To serve, cut a biscuit in half and place about ¾ cup pulled pork on top of the biscuit bottom. Drizzle some of the sauce from the pan on the pork, add coleslaw (page 35) if you are feeling adventurous, top off with the other half of the biscuit, and serve.

SERVING SUGGESTIONS: If you're a Pittsburgher or have been to the Three Rivers and eaten at Primanti's you'll love this with a bit of coleslaw from the Claw and Slaw recipe (page 35). However, you don't have to be a "Yinzer" (someone with a Pittsburgh accent) to fall in love with the slaw and pork pairing.

Ribollita

Sometimes we host a special dinner at the Market called Venti. For each Venti we bring in a different chef who prepares a menu unique to their cooking style in partnership with a local winery. One of the most popular Venti dinners was with Chef Randall Wilson, who flew in from Long Island and prepared gourmet dishes paired with sparkling wines from Equality Vines and pinot noirs from Emeritus Vineyards. When Randall told us he would be making Ribollita—a classic Tuscan vegetable stew— we asked him to prepare more. Something told us that this recipe would go well atop a biscuit. Our instincts proved to be correct. The following day we sold out of it pretty quickly. This recipe is adapted to Randall's tastes and topped with gremolata. Gremolata is a combination of fresh parsley, garlic, and lemon zest that really brings stew, sauce, and many other dishes to life. It's not hard to make, either (see below). We got lucky when Randall agreed to share this recipe with us and know you will love the end result.

Makes 6 to 8 servings

6 tablespoons extra-virgin olive oil

1 small eggplant, cut into ½-inch pieces

1 small zucchini, cut into ½-inch pieces

1 small summer squash, cut into ½-inch pieces

Kosher salt, to taste

Freshly ground black pepper, to taste

6 Yukon Gold potatoes, cut into quarters

1 small onion, chopped

1 carrot, chopped

1 celery stalk, chopped

1 tablespoon minced garlic

2 (15-ounce) cans whole peeled tomatoes

4 cups vegetable stock or water

1 fresh rosemary sprig

1 fresh thyme sprig

2 bay leaves

2 cups cannellini or butter beans, drained and rinsed

3 cups chopped kale or escarole

¼ cup thinly sliced fresh basil

6 to 8 biscuits (page 20), depending on how many you're serving

1 cup freshly grated Parmesan

For the gremolata (makes ⅓ to ½ cup):

2 cups fresh parsley

Zest from ½ lemon (about 1 teaspoon)

2 garlic cloves

Preheat the oven to 450°F.

Place 4 tablespoons of oil in a large 5-quart saucepan and heat over medium-high heat. Sauté the eggplant, zucchini, and squash until lightly browned. Season with salt and pepper.

In a separate pot, boil the potatoes until they are on the verge of fork tender. Drain and set aside.

Pour the remaining 2 tablespoons of oil in a large stock pot over medium heat. Add the onion, carrot, celery, and garlic; sprinkle with salt and pepper and cook, stirring occasionally, until the vegetables are soft, 5 to 10 minutes.

Add the tomatoes with their juices, vegetable stock, rosemary, thyme, and bay leaves. Bring to a boil, then reduce to a slow simmer; cook, stirring once or twice to break up the tomatoes, until the flavors meld, 25 to 30 minutes.

Add the beans, potatoes, kale, and the eggplant mixture. Cook for an additional 10 minutes. Scoop out the bay leaves, taste, and add salt and pepper as desired. Add fresh basil, stir to incorporate, and let cook for an additional 20 to 30 minutes.

Prepare the gremolata. Chop the parsley with the lemon zest and garlic cloves.

Ladle the Ribollita over a biscuit and top with grated Parmesan and gremolata. Then watch as the dish is devoured.

Market Vegan Marsala

The minute I learned we'd be making a cookbook we launched community dinner night at the Market. The evening became our test kitchen for the book and our friends and family in Guerneville participated in tasting many of the recipes. The Market Vegan Marsala was one the most popular recipes we tested. The mushrooms give this dish a deep and earthy flavor and the Marsala wine adds a unique flavor profile. Instead of sautéing the veggies, we opted for roasting, and made the sauce separate from the vegetables. Roasting adds even more depth and is well worth the effort.

Makes 8 servings

1 sweet yellow onion, chopped

8 cups cremini mushrooms, chopped

3 carrots, peeled and chopped

3 to 5 celery stalks, from the center of the bunch with leaves

8 baby new potatoes, cut into quarters

3 tablespoons extra-virgin olive oil

For the marsala sauce:

8 cups vegetable stock

2 cups Marsala wine

½ cup all-purpose flour

2 fresh rosemary sprigs

2 fresh thyme sprigs

2 tablespoons fresh oregano

2 tablespoons dried mustard

2 teaspoons kosher salt, plus more for taste

2 teaspoons freshly ground black pepper, plus more for taste

8 Original Big Bottom Biscuits (page 20)

Gremolata (page 120)

Preheat the oven to 350°F.

Place the onion, mushrooms, carrots, celery, and potatoes onto a cookie sheet and coat with the olive oil. Roast in the oven for 20 to 25 minutes.

While the veggies are roasting, prepare the Marsala sauce. Put vegetable broth in a stockpot on medium heat. Blend the Marsala wine and flour in a blender and slowly whisk the mixture into the heated vegetable broth. It will begin to thicken. Add in the rosemary, thyme, oregano, mustard, salt, and pepper. Transfer the roasted vegetables to the sauce and continue to cook on low to medium heat for another 25 to 30 minutes.

Taste and add additional salt and pepper as desired. Serve a ladle of Marsala sauce atop a biscuit in a gorgeous bowl and sprinkle with gremolata.

VARIATION: If you want to make it meaty, marinate six boneless chicken breasts in ½ cup Marsala wine with 2 tablespoons of olive oil and a teaspoon each of salt and pepper. Then grill the meat over medium heat for 5 minutes on each side. Remove from the grill, chop into bite-size pieces, and add into the Market Marsala with the roasted vegetables.

Save Your Vegetable Scraps!

We always have a lot of veggie scraps left over at the market—the peels from carrots, the end of onions, the bottoms of celery bundles are always bountiful in our kitchen. With food cost constantly on our minds, we encourage everyone to save anything that can be used later for veggie stock. You can do this at home too; while you may not have the volume of scraps we have, you can create a scrap bag and keep it in the freezer. I got this idea from my good friend and fellow foodie John Spear. Once you have about 6 to 8 cups of vegetable scraps you can make your own veggie stock by placing the scraps in a stock pot, covering with water, adding in 1 tablespoon each of salt and peppercorns, and letting it cook down for 45 minutes to an hour on medium heat. Add more water and continue to cook down for another hour on low heat. Use this right away or freeze for later use.

Moroccan Chicken

When we first opened the Market we tried just about everything we could do to get people through our doors. Beyond serving our regular breakfast, lunch, and deli menu, our team came up with happy hour ideas, local celebrity sandwiches, and a weekly Market dinner. Tricia Brown, technology guru and foodie, was our very first executive chef at the Market. She helped us craft our daytime menu and brought us her version of Moroccan Chicken stew that people love. Now we host a community dinner once a week and this is often on the menu. Our customers love this aromatic dish, and of course it pairs well atop—what else?—a biscuit.

Makes 6 to 8 servings

6 chicken thighs

3 tablespoons extra-virgin olive oil, plus more for drizzling on chicken

1 tablespoon kosher salt, plus more for taste

1 tablespoon freshly ground black pepper, plus more for taste

2 medium yellow onions, chopped

6 garlic cloves, minced

1 tablespoon ground coriander

1 tablespoon ground cumin

1 tablespoon ground nutmeg

1 tablespoon paprika

1 teaspoon turmeric

¼ cup honey

¼ of a preserved lemon, chopped (you can buy preserved lemon at a gourmet grocery story or skip it if you cannot find a jar)

4 cups peeled and sliced carrots

2 cups chopped celery

2 cups chopped whole fennel

1 cup pitted green or black olives (I prefer the green Castelvetrano olives or black Kalamatas)

6 cups vegetable stock

Cilantro and lime wedges, for garnish

6 to 8 biscuits (page 20)

Preheat the oven to 350°F.

Place the chicken thighs on a cookie sheet and drizzle with oil and 1 tablespoon each of salt and pepper. Bake in the oven for 15 to 20 minutes. Remove, cover, and set aside to cool. Once cool, chop into bite-size pieces. You'll add these to the stockpot later.

Heat the 3 tablespoons oil in a large heavy pot over medium-high heat. Add onions and sauté until translucent, 3 to 5 minutes. Stir in the garlic, coriander, cumin, nutmeg, paprika, turmeric, honey, and preserved lemon, and cook until fragrant and well combined, 1 to 2 minutes. Add in the carrots, celery, fennel, and olives and continue to cook until the vegetables are tender, stirring frequently as the veggies cook.

Reduce the heat to medium and add in vegetable stock and chicken and cook for another 10 to 15 minutes. Season to taste with salt and pepper. Spoon the stew over a biscuit and garnish with cilantro sprigs and a lime wedge.

VARIATION: This dish can also be made without the chicken to make it vegetarian. Just up the amount of carrots, celery, and fennel by 1 cup each and you'll have a hearty and delicious veggie Moroccan stew.

Asian Ahi Tuna Salad

In the spring and summer I spend time in Fire Island Pines sharing a house with a group of guys that I've known for years. We've hosted numerous dinner parties and cook a lot of delicious food together in one of the most magical places in the world. Bruce, our local butcher and fishmonger, always has the freshest cuts and catches of the day. So when I was noodling on recipe ideas for an Asian tuna salad, I chatted with Bruce and he just happened to have a big piece of fresh ahi tuna that I used for this recipe. While you can always find high-quality canned tuna, try using freshly caught ahi if you can; you won't be disappointed.

Makes 4 to 5 cups

2 to 3 tablespoons extra-virgin olive oil
2 to 2½ pounds fresh ahi tuna
3 tablespoons sour cream
3 teaspoons black sesame seeds
3 teaspoons soy sauce
2 teaspoons chopped fresh ginger
3 teaspoons wasabi powder or paste
9 biscuits (page 20)

Over medium heat, cover the bottom of a large saucepan with the oil and sear the fish on both sides until cooked through, 3 to 5 minutes. Set aside.

Whisk the remaining ingredients, except the biscuits, in a large bowl. Taste and adjust salt level by adding additional soy sauce. You can also pump up the heat by adding more wasabi powder. If you like your tuna salad a little creamier, add more mayonnaise or sour cream (depending on your tastes). Split a biscuit in half, top with the tuna salad, and serve with a side of mixed greens tossed with Cumin Vinaigrette (page 85).

Simple and Hearty Vegan Stew

In the winter months we bring the community together one night a week and serve up tasty stews with a biscuit, side salad, and hearty glass of Big Bottom Market wine. This is one of our favorite community dinner meals and we always make a little extra to serve up the following day. On our community dinner nights we have a make-it-meaty option. We always prepare a vegetarian or vegan stew as the base and then roast or grill meats as an add-on. I personally love this dish with seasoned and grilled strips of flank steak—and many of our guests love it this way too!

Makes 6 servings

2 tablespoons extra-virgin olive oil

3 garlic cloves, chopped (about 1 tablespoon)

1 large yellow onion, chopped

2 fennel bulbs, chopped (fronds reserved)

4 stalks celery, chopped

3 carrots, peeled and chopped

2 red bell peppers, cored, seeded, and chopped

1 cup dry white wine

1 teaspoon fresh thyme

1 teaspoon fresh basil

1 teaspoon celery seed

1 teaspoon oregano

½ teaspoon crushed red pepper flakes

2 tablespoons fennel fronds

½ teaspoon kosher salt

½ teaspoon freshly ground black pepper

2 (28-ounce) cans Italian peeled tomatoes

½ cup parsley, chopped

6 Original Big Bottom Biscuits (page 20)

Place a medium saucepan over medium heat and cover the bottom of the pan with the oil. Add in the garlic and onion and sauté for 2 to 3 minutes, or until the onions are translucent. Add in the fennel, celery, carrots, and bell peppers and continue to cook for an additional 5 minutes. Turn the heat to high; after about a minute, add in white wine, scrape the bottom with a wooden spoon or spatula to remove anything that is stuck to the bottom (this is referred to as deglazing the pan) and let cook down to half.

Add in the thyme, basil, celery seed, oregano, pepper flakes, fennel fronds, salt, and pepper and continue to sauté for another minute, ensuring that the spices are evenly distributed.

Blend the tomatoes with an immersion blender or food processor and add into the pan. Cook for another 20 minutes. Right before serving, add in the chopped parsley.

Serve with a biscuit, of course. You can either serve the stew over the biscuit or dunk your biscuit right in the bowl.

VARIATION: If you want to add meat to this dish, season 2 pounds of flank steak with salt, pepper, and a liberal coating of olive oil. Refrigerate for about an hour to allow the spices and oil to marinate the meat. Get an outdoor or stove-top grill really hot and sear the meat on both sides for 3 to 5 minutes, depending on how you like your meat cooked. Slice thinly and serve the grilled steak on top of each bowl.

Mediterranean Spiced Chicken with Tzatziki

This recipe was inspired by a trip to Oman where spices are used abundantly and effortlessly in many of their dishes. It also includes a recipe from the Conomos family—great friends, neighbors, and foodies—who have taught me so much about Greek cooking. When I asked Janet, the matriarch and flawless entertainer, about tzatziki, she pointed me to her daughter, who showed me the right way to make this Greek staple. The resulting combination is magical and makes a great biscuit sandwich. You'll use half of the tzatziki for this recipe; the other half can be stored in an airtight container in the refrigerator for about 1 week and makes for a great appetizer. Serve with Kalamata olives, some feta cheese, and the Mini Biscuit (page 22) at your next cocktail party.

Makes 9 servings

9 biscuits (page 20)
9 chicken thighs
2 tablespoons extra-virgin olive oil
1 tablespoon honey
½ teaspoon kosher salt
½ teaspoon freshly ground black pepper

For the spice mix:
1 tablespoon paprika
1 tablespoon cumin
1 tablespoon ground ginger
1 tablespoon turmeric
1 teaspoon dried mustard
1 teaspoon celery seed
½ teaspoon cayenne pepper
½ teaspoon ground cinnamon

For Ali's tzatziki:
3 cucumbers, peeled, seeded, and chopped
2 teaspoons kosher salt, plus more to taste
1 (35-ounce) container plain Greek yogurt
1 medium garlic clove, minced
1 tablespoon extra-virgin olive oil
1 teaspoon oregano
1 teaspoon fresh mint
1 teaspoon fresh dill
1 tablespoon honey
2 teaspoons freshly ground black pepper, plus more to taste
¼ cup fresh lemon juice (1 lemon)

Preheat the oven to 350°F.

Prepare the spice mixture by combining all the ingredients in a large bowl and stir well. You'll use half of the mixture for this recipe and the other half can be stored in an airtight container in the freezer. I always make extra at home and use it to flavor other meat and veggie dishes as well as salad dressings.

Place the chicken thighs in a large bowl and add in half the spice mixture, the oil, honey, salt, and pepper. Stir well, making sure to mix everything together while coating the thighs evenly.

Transfer the chicken thighs to a large baking dish, spacing them out evenly so they aren't crowded. Put the baking dish into the oven for 15 to 20 minutes. Remove, use a meat thermometer to ensure doneness (the thermometer should read 165°F), and set aside.

While the chicken is cooking, prepare the tzatziki. Start by sprinkling 2 teaspoons of salt on the cucumbers and coat evenly. Wrap the cucumber in cheesecloth and squeeze the liquid out of the wrapped cucumbers until all the liquid is gone.

Combine the yogurt, cucumbers, and the remaining ingredients in a bowl and mix well. Add salt to taste.

To serve, cut the biscuits in half. Spread a little bit of tzatziki on the bottom of the biscuit and place the thigh on top. Add more tzatziki to your chicken, put the top on, and serve.

Note that I have slightly adjusted Ali's recipe for more simplicity. Ali uses cheesecloth to squeeze out all the liquid from her cucumbers and lets them sit overnight in a sieve in the refrigerator. This gives the final version a thicker consistency. I like my consistency a little thinner so I use the cheesecloth and skip the overnight stay in the refrigerator.

Colonel Armstrong
Curry Chicken Salad

This is another Market favorite and if we ever even thought of taking it off the menu our regulars would chase us out of town. For years we used to make this with breast meat only, but being fans of both dark and white meats, we decided to add in thighs as well. The result is pretty tasty, and when served on a biscuit, life is even better.

Makes 9 servings

4 cups cooked and chopped chicken thighs and breast meat (from about 1 pound boneless breasts and 1 pound boneless thighs)

1 cup chopped green apple with skin on (about ½ an apple)

¾ cup mayonnaise

⅓ cup chopped cilantro

¼ cup chopped roasted and salted cashews

¼ cup currants or raisins

¼ cup chopped shallots

1½ tablespoons chopped fresh mint

2 tablespoons yellow curry powder (see note)

2 tablespoons honey

9 biscuits (page 20)

After prepping the ingredients, combine everything in a large bowl and mix well. It really is that easy!

NOTES: There is no salt in this recipe. The saltiness will come from the mayonnaise and cashews. You can add more salt, but make sure you taste the finished product first. As my mother says, you can always add more if you need it, but you cannot take away.

For simplicity's sake, we use yellow curry powder in this recipe at the Market, which is absolutely delicious. Personally, I am a fan of making my own curry powder. It's not too time-consuming and you can make a bunch and store it in an airtight container in the freezer to ensure freshness (recipe follows).

Yellow Curry Powder

Makes about 1 to 1½ cups

5 tablespoons coriander seeds

2 tablespoons cumin seeds

1½ tablespoons black peppercorns

1 teaspoon whole cloves

1½ tablespoons whole cardamom pods

1 cinnamon stick, about 2 inches long

1½ tablespoons crushed red pepper flakes

3 tablespoons dried turmeric

4 teaspoons ground ginger

In a saucepan over low heat, toast the coriander, cumin, peppercorns, cloves, cardamom, cinnamon stick, and pepper flakes for about 2 minutes. You'll need to stir constantly to keep the whole spices from getting too toasty. The room will fill with wonderful aromas and a bit of smoke will emit from the pan. Remove and place into a blender, spice grinder, or food processor. Add in the turmeric and ginger and grind until the mixture has turned into a powder. Transfer to an airtight container and store in the freezer for maximum freshness. This will keep for up to 6 months.

HOST YOUR OWN
"BISCUIT BAR" PARTY

When we popped up in New York City we called our little venture the Big Bottom Biscuit Bar. While the pop-up only lasted for a short time in the Big Apple, the biscuit bar concept stuck and our team often replicates various versions at homes and businesses all over Sonoma County and beyond.

The options for a biscuit bar are endless and range from breakfast sweets to lunch and dinnertime savory items. There are two items that are consistently available at any biscuit bar: the biscuits are bountiful, and we always make sure the sparkling wine is flowing freely for those wanting to imbibe.

Here are tips for setting up your own biscuit bar right at home:

✦ Our general manager and operating partner Donna always recommends that you have enough for two biscuits per person at any event. While most people will eat only one, there will always be a few who go for more; any leftovers can be used to make your own Biscuit Pie Crust (page 148).

✦ You'll want to have about 2 ounces of smoked salmon per person and arrange the fish on a simple white platter garnished with lemons and some parsley for color.

✦ Be sure to have crème fraîche, pickled onions (page 34), and capers as well. We usually plan for 1½ to 2 tablespoons of each per person and present them on the buffet in large ramekins with serving utensils for each.

✦ The same 1½ to 2 tablespoons per person also works for jams and butters. We like to have two to three options for both jams and butters. Guests love a little variety, and when served in lovely antique mismatched bowls, your table will not only look gorgeous but also bountiful.

+ Local honey is a must and looks perfect when presented on the table in a honey pot with a wooden dipper.

+ To ensure variety and satisfy those who may want to pass on the gluten, you'll want to create a fruit salad. Plan for about 3/4 cup per person and choose a mix of fruits including melons, strawberries, blueberries, oranges, and bananas. You can also give your fruit salad a sweet zing by squeezing some lime juice and drizzling honey over the top before you serve. For every 2 to 3 cups of fruit salad, squeeze the juice from 1 lime on top along with about a tablespoon of honey. Serve this in a big see-through glass bowl. The colors will add to your overall tablescape.

+ Yogurt is another must and Greek is our favorite. Plan for about 1/2 cup to 3/4 cup per guest and present on the table in a beautiful bowl along with a wooden serving spoon.

+ We make homemade granola at the Market and our customers love to add this as another option on their buffet tables. You can make your own (there are a number of recipes online) or head to your local gourmet store and pick some up. The world is filled with artisanal granola, and if you are planning a party and want to make it easy on yourself, a store-bought version, removed from the packaging and served in a beautiful bowl, will work just fine.

+ Make sure to have juices, sparkling water, and still water for guests. We love to put bowls of sliced grapefruit and oranges next to a classic bar juicer and let people squeeze their own fruit and serve themselves. You can also buy freshly squeezed juices and transfer to glass pitchers for the table. We always avoid putting branded plastic and glass bottles on the buffet. Find yourself some old glass milk jugs or antique pitchers and transfer your nonalcoholic drinks into these for serving.

+ Last and certainly not least are the bubbles. We prefer to serve sparkling wine from the Russian River (our favorite is the Love Wins from Equality Vines or anything that Iron Horse Vineyards makes), but if you're a traditionalist and love Champagne, then go for the gold with a bottle of Billecart or any other favorite producer from France. You can go classic on glassware and use Champagne flutes along with rocks glasses, or get some small cafe tumblers. We love this look, because it matches perfectly with our overall Market style.

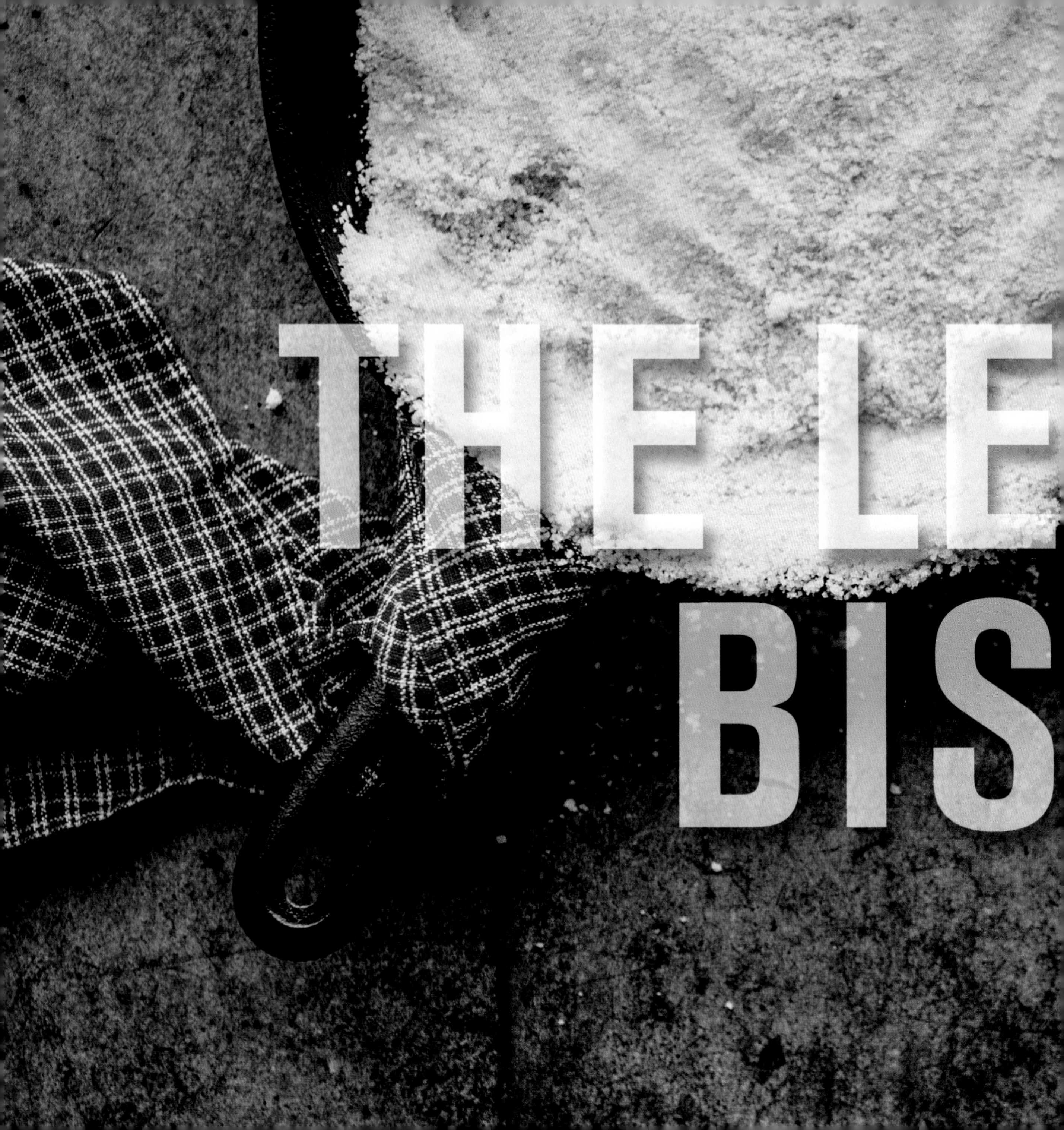
THE LE
BIS

It's rare, but it happens. Sometimes there are leftover biscuits, and since it's a shame to waste good food, our team has come up with delicious ways to utilize what is left over. Because many of our leftover biscuit recipes have become staples at the Market we often make additional plain biscuits so we can transform them into pies, tarts, quiches, and much more.

MAKING BISCUIT DUST

If you have leftover biscuits, make sure to wrap them securely in plastic wrap and store in the freezer. Your leftover biscuits will last about three months in the freezer. When ready to use, pull out of the freezer and turn them into what we at the market call biscuit dust. Biscuit dust is the base for all of our pies, tarts, quiches, and pot pies.

To make your dust, let biscuits thaw if needed. Crumble about four to five into the bowl of a food processor and pulse until completely and uniformly pulverized. Voilà. You'll have about 4 cups of biscuit dust and are now ready to get cooking.

To store biscuit dust, put into a large sealable bag or airtight container and place in the refrigerator for up to 5 days. Use in the recipes in this chapter.

Biscuit Pie Crust

If you have some biscuit dust on hand, biscuit pie crust is a snap to make. It can be used for so many great recipes or as a complete replacement for traditional pie crust. The result is incredibly versatile and works in both sweet and savory dishes. Making the crust is a hands-on endeavor, or what I like to call "digital cooking." Using your hands in the cooking process not only gives you an actual feel for the texture of the food, but the ingredients will feel the love coming from your fingertips.

Makes 1 crust

4 to 5 cups biscuit dust (page 146)

Preheat the oven to 350°F. Coat a 9½-inch baking pan or pie plate with cooking spray.

Pour the biscuit dust into the baking pan or pie plate. You can also use a large bowl and your hands to break up the biscuits into tiny little pieces. Using your fingers, press the biscuits into the bottom and sides of the pan until all areas are covered.

Bake in the oven for 20 to 25 minutes, or until golden brown.

Your biscuit pie crust is ready! Now get cooking with some of the leftover biscuit recipes.

Strawberry Cream Cheese Crumble

This is a Theresa creation and a bestseller at the Market. I think people love this one so much, because it is very decadent and has layers of flavor. The richness of the cream cheese frosting pairs with the sweet strawberries and is held together with the eggs. The crumble tops it off, with every bite just melting in your mouth. We highly suggest serving this one with a scoop of vanilla ice cream or fresh whipped cream and a glass of Russian River Chardonnay.

Makes 6 to 8 slices

1 Biscuit Pie Crust (page 148)

For the cream cheese frosting:

8 ounces cream cheese, at room temperature

2 cups confectioners' sugar

1 teaspoon vanilla extract

¼ cup heavy cream

For the crumble topping:

6 tablespoons unsalted butter, at room temperature

1 cup all-purpose flour

½ cup light brown sugar

1 teaspoon ground cinnamon

For the pie filling:

4 cups chopped strawberries

4 large eggs

½ cup granulated sugar

Preheat the oven to 350°F.

Fit your standing mixer with a paddle. To make the cream cheese frosting, combine the cream cheese, confectioners' sugar, vanilla extract, and cream in the mixing bowl. Turn on low to keep the sugar from flying all over the place and slowly turn up the speed until the ingredients are well combined. Set aside.

For the crumble topping, mix the butter, flour, brown sugar, and cinnamon until well combined and set aside.

Spread the cream cheese frosting on the bottom of the pie crust and add the strawberries. Whip the eggs with ½ cup granulated sugar and pour over the top. Poke a skewer into the top of the pie to allow the eggs to seep into the crust. Top with the crumble mixture and bake in the oven for about 30 minutes. Once the pie is done, let cool and slice (or scoop out of the pan) for serving.

Biscuit Berry Apple Crumble

This crumble recipe reminds me of my mother's cooking. When we had an abundance of fruit in the kitchen, usually around holiday time when the kitchen was overflowing with fruit baskets, she would get creative and make all sorts of crumbles. This berry apple version is easy to make and cooks up pretty quickly. Keep in mind that the crust is not as dense as a regular pie crust. When you cut into this crumble, it literally crumbles. Serve in a shallow bowl with a scoop of French vanilla ice cream or a dollop of whipped cream. This dish also goes well with lemon curd (page 61) on top, which adds a sweet and tart flavor to every bite.

Makes 6 slices

2 cups biscuit dust
2 medium green apples, skins on
1½ cups chopped strawberries
1½ cups blueberries
2 cups light brown sugar
½ cup fresh lemon juice (2 lemons)
3 tablespoons all-purpose flour

Preheat the oven to 350°F.

Coat a 9-inch tart pan with cooking spray and then firmly press the two cups of biscuit dust into the pan until the entire bottom and sides are well covered. Place into the oven and cook for 15 to 20 minutes, or until golden brown. Remove and set aside.

Thinly slice the apples and place into a mixing bowl (we use a mandoline to get really thin slices). Add in the strawberries, blueberries, brown sugar, lemon juice, and flour. Mix well until all ingredients are well combined.

Pour ingredients into the baked tart crust and place back into the oven. Let cook for about 20 minutes and check for doneness. Your apples should be slightly brown and the mixture of juices from the fruit, lemon juice, sugar, and flour should be bubbly.

Remove from the oven to cool and then serve each slice with your favorite vanilla ice cream.

Zucchini Quiche
with Asiago and Parmesan

Biscuit quiche has become a staple at the Market. We used to only serve quiches on the weekends, but the demand far outweighed the supply so we started making them more regularly. The zucchini has a light and delicate flavor that pairs well with the richness of the Asiago and Parmesan cheeses. This is a dish that screams for a small side salad with some Champagne vinaigrette. While you are at it, you may also want to pour yourself a glass of sparkling wine from the Russian River Valley or your favorite Champagne. What's breakfast without bubbles?

Makes 6 to 8 slices

4 to 5 cups biscuit dust (page 146)

2 tablespoons extra-virgin olive oil

½ large onion

1 tablespoon chopped garlic

2 to 3 medium zucchinis, quartered and chopped

¼ cup dry vermouth

12 large eggs

1 cup buttermilk

1 cup grated Asiago

1 cup grated Parmesan

½ cup chopped fresh parsley

½ teaspoon crushed red pepper flakes

1 teaspoon kosher salt

1 teaspoon freshly ground black pepper

Preheat the oven to 375°F.

In a 9 x 13-inch baking dish or iron skillet, press the biscuit dust into the bottom and onto the sides until the entire surface is covered. Place into the oven for 15 to 20 minutes, until golden brown. Remove and set aside.

Place the oil in a large saucepan over medium heat. Sauté the onion and garlic until translucent, 2 to 3 minutes. Add the zucchinis and turn the heat to high. As the pan gets even hotter, add in the vermouth and let cook down by half. Remove the pan from the heat and set aside to cool.

Beat the eggs in a separate bowl and add in the remaining ingredients. Stir well and then add in the zucchini mixture. Pour this mixture into your prepared crust and place back into the oven for another 30 to 35 minutes. Remove from the oven and test with a toothpick, skewer, or knife to ensure that the quiche has cooked through. If it does not come out clean or egg mixture leaks out, place back into the oven for another 5 to 10 minutes until done.

VARIATION: If you want to make this one meaty, then add in 2 cups of cooked mild or hot Italian sausage.

Foraged Mushroom Biscuit Quiche

Living in western Sonoma County is pretty amazing. From the wineries and redwoods to the Russian River emptying into the Pacific Ocean, we have access to so much beauty and nature. Our good friends Matt and Barb Gustafson, the owners of Paul Mathew Winery, turned us onto mushroom foraging and each year they host a foraging event in the hills of Cazadero. For a few hours a group roams around staring at the ground hoping to come across a handful of Black Trumpets or Chanterelles. It takes a lot of concentration and if you are lucky you'll find more than enough edible fungi to make an amazing meal. We realize of course that not everyone can forage for mushrooms, but you can forage at your local gourmet grocery store for your favorite kinds. For this recipe choose the type that you love best. Cremini, Shiitake, Chanterelle—the options are endless. If you do decide to forage for mushroom, make sure you take someone who knows what to look for. While many mushrooms in the wild are absolutely delicious, many are extremely poisonous and in some cases deadly. So, please forage with caution and with an expert.

Makes 6 to 8 slices

2 tablespoons extra-virgin olive oil

3 garlic cloves, minced

1 sweet yellow onion, chopped

1 cup dry white wine

2 cups chopped mushrooms
(a mix of your favorites works well)

1 (14-ounce) can diced tomatoes

1 cup shredded sharp white cheddar cheese

8 large eggs, beaten

1 teaspoon kosher salt

1 teaspoon freshly ground black pepper

1 Biscuit Pie Crust (page 148),
fully baked and cooled

Place the oil in a medium saucepan over medium heat. Add in the garlic and onion and sauté for 2 to 3 minutes, until the onions are translucent. Add in the wine and mushrooms and continue to sauté until the wine has cooked down all the way. Add in the tomatoes and continue to cook for 5 minutes. Set aside and let cool for 15 to 20 minutes and then add in the cheese, eggs, salt, and pepper and stir until well mixed.

Pour into the crust and bake for about 30 minutes. The top should be golden brown; when a toothpick comes out clean your quiche is done. If it doesn't come out clean, leave the quiche in the oven for a few more minutes and test again.

Biscuit Chicken Pot Pie

Whenever we make these pot pies they disappear almost immediately. Combining the leftover biscuit crust with our veggie gravy gives this dish a sublime richness that literally warms the soul. The greatest thing about this recipe is that it freezes beautifully. So you can make it, freeze it, pull out, and reheat when you are ready for a tasty meal.

Makes 6 pot pies

6 boneless chicken thighs

3 to 5 baby red potatoes, chopped (about 1½ cups)

7 cups biscuit crumbles

2 tablespoons extra-virgin olive oil

1 medium onion, chopped (about 1½ cups)

3 large carrots, peeled and diced (about 1½ cups)

3 celery stalks, diced (about 1½ cups)

½ cup chicken broth

2 cups vegetarian gravy (page 109)

Paprika, for garnish

Preheat the oven to 350°F.

Place the chicken thighs on a baking sheet and cook for 10 minutes, rotate the pan, and then continue cooking for another 10 to 15 minutes. Check to make sure they are done, remove, and set aside. Leave the oven on.

Rinse the chopped potatoes under cold water to remove excess starch. Place potatoes into a medium pot and add water until covered. Cook over high heat until potatoes are done, but not mushy. Set aside.

While the chicken and potatoes are cooking, spray the insides of six medium ramekins or bowls with cooking spray. Place 1 cup biscuit crumble into each of the ramekins and firmly press the crumbles with your fingertips into the sides to form the crust. Set additional crumbles aside.

Add the oil to the bottom of a medium stockpot and sauté the onions until translucent, 3 to 5 minutes. Add the carrots, celery, and chicken broth, and continue to cook, covered, for 5 more minutes.

Chop the chicken into bite-size pieces and add to the stockpot with the potatoes and vegetarian gravy. Continue to cook until the mixture starts to boil.

Scoop about 1½ cups of the mixture into each of the ramekins and top with leftover biscuit crumbles. Sprinkle a bit of paprika on the top of each pot pie and bake for 10 minutes. Remove and serve.

A NOTE ON THE PHOTOGRAPHY

The photographs in this book were conceived and taken by the amazingly talented Kelly Puleio. Her work graces the pages of many cocktail books and cookbooks and it only made sense to bring her in on this project.

As Donna Prowse, our operating partner and general manager, and I were planning the photo shoot we made a conscious decision to ensure that friends, family, and employees of the market had a hand in helping Kelly make her photos beautiful.

Faviana Priola, our funky friend with an eye for design and the owner of a lovely store called Dazzle in Portland, Oregon, helped us shop for platters, plates, and gorgeous utensils right here in Sonoma County.

My close friends and talented designers Matthew Jernigan and Rachel Hoopes helped us style the photos focusing on the redwood chic theme we were going for. Theresa Bernabe—our chef and the woman who pumps food out of our small kitchen every single day—along with Sue Steiner—the Market momma—cooked up a storm on the days of the photo shoot.

Special thanks goes out to this team of friends and family for pitching in, helping out, and making this book absolutely beautiful. Love you all.

ACKNOWLEDGMENTS

This book would not be possible without the support from so many friends and family.

My parents, Ray and Sharon Volpatt, taught me so much about the importance of food and family. My brother, Ray Jr., and sister, Amy Connors, who continue to reinforce the importance of food in our daily lives along with their spouses Tracy Volpatt and Chris Connors, and children (my nieces and nephews) Sam, Maggie, Lucy, and Nicholas are all an inspiration.

My grandparents, who inspired me in many ways and always loved me. You keep looking down and sending me positive energy.

If you know me, you have heard about my cousin Lou Lou who passed away from ovarian cancer. She still sends me pennies from heaven and inspires me through her husband PJ (an amazing cook in his own right). My other cousins, Carol, Biz, and Paul, and their spouses/partners, children, and grandchildren.

The Market would not be possible if it weren't for my business partner Kate Larkin, who supported this venture from the beginning and has elegantly weathered every storm as we continue to drive toward even more success.

Our operating partner, Donna Prowse, makes the machine run and keeps everything in check. We love you.

The entire team at the Market pitches in almost daily to keep us humming along. I would be remiss not to call out Arturo, who has been with us since the beginning, and Theresa, the woman who cranks more food out of our tiny kitchen than anyone else. She played such an important role in recipe testing and idea generation.

My agent, Joelle Delbourgo, who bought into this project from the get-go. I would have never met her had it not been for Jim Obergefell who I am not only thankful to have in my life, but is one of the people that helped change SCOTUS history and marriage equality for the LGBTQ community.

My "sisters" Courtney Benedict and Heather Terrell have rooted this project on from day one. I am lucky to have known you for as long as I have.

The chosen Guerneville family Heidi, Brian, Deneene, Chris, Christian, Brian, Debbie, and Steve, and my brother from another mother and business partner, Matt.

Sean and David, you are crazy and I love it. Whether we are traveling or sitting still (never) in Guerneville, we are always having fun.

Oh Faviana and Dale, you are crazy and you love me unconditionally and that means the world to me.

Tricia and Kerry. Tricia, you are always there with a pairing recommendation or as a recipe consult when needed. Kerry, you are my favorite woman with a complete toolbox. It's been a great ride with both and I am so happy we are close!

Jeffrey Lais, you inspire me, and to think it all started at a graduation party. Katie Geminder, thanks for joining me in some amazing world travels that have inspired our cooking adventures.

The Guerneville community at large continues to support our efforts along with the mothers and fathers with Friends of Guerneville School.

John Spear, you are a wealth of food knowledge, and Anders Nelson, you always clean up. I would have never met Steve and Dan and learned the wonders of leftover turkey pot pie had it not been for you two.

Ken, Grant, Jay, and the San Diego crew. Thanks for letting me into the circle and always including me.

Ronnie, I would not be "normal" and comfortable in my own skin if we hadn't become friends and learned how to be ourselves.

Lance Larsh, you are the best master baker I know. I did my best to channel your meticulousness as I tested each and every recipe.

Jim, Jim, Darren, Kirby, Chuck, and Judy, you all inspire me and I love our life and times on Fire Island. Food and friends I will never forget.

Brian Perrin, you encouraged me from the beginning, and when things looked good, then not so good, then good again, you jumped in, advised, and were always an advocate.

Jim and Anthony, ever so willing to jump in at the last minute to lend a helping hand with an eye for sharp design.

Crista, thanks so much for your vision and hard work in helping to get this Market on its feet.

All of my boys on Midway, Beach Hill, Tarpon, and Crown, we have eaten a lot of food and have had a lot of fun together.

Marimar Torres, you are a BFF and a beautifully talented woman. Thank you.

Mary and Dave, you've both been an inspiration and great mentors from the beginning of my career. I love you.

INDEX

Note: Page references in *italics* indicate photographs.